Gary Henderson is a reporter's reporter. With meticulous detail, he takes the reader with him as he unravels Susan Smith's story. He captures the community's support for Smith when the troubled young woman first reported her sons' disappearance, then, the gradual skepticism many people had about her story, and finally, the horror and anger when the children were pulled out of the lake. I was one of the out-of-town reporters on the scene who grabbed the *HERALD-JOURNAL* each morning to see what Henderson and his team had uncovered. I'm just glad he wasn't working for one of my network competitors.

— Randall Pinkston
Correspondent, CBS NEWS

Those of us who have spent years reporting the news of upstate South Carolina see the Susan Smith story in a very personal way because this community is our home. Gary Henderson feels this, too. He writes from the perspective not only of a reporter, but also of a father and concerned member of the community. His book echoes the emotional rise and fall so many of us experienced those nine days in Union.

— Tom Crabtree
News Anchor, WSPA-TV

D1604396

i

Nine Days In Union

The Search for
Alex and Michael Smith

By Gary Henderson

Honoribus Press
Spartanburg, South Carolina

Published by
THE HONORIBUS PRESS
POST OFFICE BOX 4872
SPARTANBURG, SC 29305

An HONORIBUS PRESS
NON-FICTION BOOK

Printed by Altman Printing Co., Inc.
Line Art by Rob Cook   Cover Design by Lee Altman

DEDICATION

This book is dedicated to my son Marc Gary Henderson and my daughter Heather Maria Henderson. May you and the children of the world always be safe and live in peace.

American Fast Photo

CONTENTS

ACKNOWLEDGEMENTS

I am grateful to my family members, friends and colleagues who helped me with this book. Without them, I could not have written *Nine Days in Union – The Search for Alex and Michael Smith*.

Five of the people who assisted me deserve a special word of thanks. They are:

Carmela Henderson, my wife and confidant, who encouraged me to write this account, helped edit portions of the manuscript, believed in me and often brought my dinner to the *Herald-Journal* newsroom when I was covering this news story in the fall of 1994; John Lane, friend, poet, essayist and Wofford College creative writing professor who said "Just tell the story"; Betsy Teter, friend, fellow writer, former *Herald-Journal* Business Editor and Editor-in-Chief for this book, who guided me through four hard months of writing; Ed Hall of Honoribus Press, who believed in this project from the beginning and supported me; and Lee Altman, whose assistance in layout, design and printing will never be forgotten.

I would also like to thank the Spartanburg *Herald-Journal* for permission to use the articles and photographs in this book.

Many other people have influenced my life and my career

as a journalist. While I cannot list them all, or even remember some of them, I am thankful for all of you. Several who played a role in the writing of this book are listed here:

Scott Kearns, who once gave me the opportunity to prove myself; Ann Hicks, friend and trusted advisor, who is always willing to listen; Winston Hardegree, friend, writer and cultivator of wonderful gardens; and Mack Amick, friend and "agent."

But perhaps the one who was most important was Anna Mitchell, my sixth grade school teacher. She taught me to love books, told me I had a gift, and helped me unwrap it.

– Gary Henderson
Spartanburg, South Carolina
May 19, 1995

FORWARD

It's Mother's Day today. At lunch the people eating at the next table in the Cracker Barrel, a home cooking restaurant out on the Interstate, were talking about Alex and Michael Smith. "Somebody would have had to kill me to take my babies," a mother said. The table became quiet. Even the tea glasses stopped clinking for a moment. The tragedy of the needless deaths of Michael and Alex Smith the year before is still raw in upstate South Carolina. Even the mention of it feels like winter rain in your face.

Gary Henderson's *Nine Days in Union* tells a local reporter's story of possibly the two ultimate southern tragedies: the death of a family and the shaking of a small rural community to its very roots. Henderson's story might not be so compelling if he, himself, were not from upstate South Carolina. Like the four main characters in his non-fiction narrative account of the Union tragedy – little Michael and Alex, Susan and David Smith – Henderson has an attachment to upstate South Carolina and his sense of loss runs deep. He has two children; he too is a *local*. His local function is served well by this book. Gary Henderson is both newspaper reporter and chronicler of the nine days of daily turmoil making up what we can only hope will prove a once-in-a-lifetime media crime event for our small corner of South Carolina.

As a general assignment reporter for the Spartanburg *Herald-Journal*, Henderson is no stranger to the tragic and sometimes surprising world of rural, suburban and urban family violence, illness and accident. As he tells us in the opening pages, the story of Alex and Michael Smith "was the fourth tragic story about young people I'd covered in 1994." Local tragedies, all but one.

I would not be writing this forward were this a purely local story. As we all know, soon after Alex and Michael disappeared in late October an airborne battalion of national media descended on Union county – CNN, CBS, NBC, ABC, and all the major news agencies and wire services. For a week, the square in Union was the centerpiece of most homes until the bizarre closure of the story.

Gary Henderson suggests that from the very beginning, everyone in Union could sense a shaky, evolving story with more complexity than the simple one Susan Smith had told the sheriff: a young woman's two small children had been kidnapped along with the car she was driving the night before.

Henderson was the first to break many of the most important print stories in the next nine days. These stories have been printed as an appendix at the end of the book. Henderson's twelve stories alone would make for an interesting and thorough account of "the nine days in Union," but what's left out of the news accounts is the tragedy of the "I," – the first person account denied by the more "objective" newspaper style.

If you want to know the "truth" about the Susan Smith tragedy, don't listen too intently to the details of the trial soon to proceed in Union, South Carolina. Read Henderson's account of how the story unfolded according to a local reporter who covered the case.

– John Lane
Spartanburg, South Carolina
May 14, 1995

DAY I

October 26, 1994

The eastern sky showed the first signs of daylight as I walked across my front lawn and picked up the morning newspaper. I stopped and inhaled the crisp October morning. Autumn was turning upstate South Carolina golden.

It's going to be a nice day to go down to the farm, I thought, remembering a 9 a.m. assignment I had near Pauline, South Carolina, a small rural community near Spartanburg. The changing leaves would be pretty.

Photographer Mike Bonner and I were scheduled to do a routine feature story about a man who trained border collies to work with the cattle on his farm. It was a day to slip into the jeans and leave the necktie at home.

"Listen to this," I said to my wife, Carmela, as I sat down at the dining room table. "A woman was carjacked last night in Union and her children were kidnapped."

We had some conversation about how no place was safe any longer and I continued reading the short story *Herald-Journal* police beat reporter Heather Brooke had written late the night before.

"Union County sheriff's deputies were looking for a man who carjacked a woman's Mazda Protegé with her two small children in it late Tuesday night.

'Susan Vaughn Smith was heading east on Highway 49 when she stopped at a red light at Monarch Mills, about 9:15 p.m., and a man jumped into the passenger seat,' said Hugh Munn, spokesman for the State Law Enforcement Division.

'The man forced her to drive off at gunpoint,' Munn said. 'Her 3-year-old and 14-month-old children were still in the car.'"

Munn went on to say it was unclear how the mother escaped, but said she ran to a nearby house to seek assistance.

Heather had learned of the reported carjacking when she made a regular call, just before 10 p.m., to 911 communications centers in the several counties covered by the *Herald-Journal*. When she asked a Union County dispatcher "if anything was going on down there," she received this reply:

"Yes, we surely do have something going on tonight."

Knowing she had a 10:30 p.m. deadline for our first edition, the best Heather could do was write a "brief," and let reporters follow the story the next morning. When she left work that night, she began a scheduled one-week vacation. The breaking story was the only one Heather wrote about Susan Smith.

As I showered and dressed on Wednesday morning, I could not get the story about the mother and her children off my mind. I dressed hurriedly and reached the office shortly after 7:30 a.m.

"I think we have a big one on our hands," I said to Scott Kearns, the *Herald-Journal* managing editor, as he walked through the newsroom. Scott, a 49-year-old graying man who some people say looks like Johnny Carson, is a veteran newspaper man with a keen sense of what makes a good story. He has judgment that can be trusted.

"Yes, we do," he replied. "Come into my office."

I logged off my computer terminal and followed him. Photographer Mike Bonner was right behind me.

Scott was already on the phone, trying to locate Ralph Greer, the newspaper's Union bureau reporter. Instead, he found Ralph's wife who told him Ralph was already at the sheriff's office at the Union County Courthouse.

"We're going to need two reporters down there today," Scott said as he dialed the telephone number to activate Ralph's beeper. "As soon as you finish in Pauline, go straight to Union."

By the time he'd finished his conversation with Ralph Greer, our orders for the day had changed.

"We'll get Pauline reassigned," Scott said. "Meet Ralph at the courthouse in Union."

Bonner and I turned and headed for his burgundy Nissan van.

Over the next two weeks, Bonner and I would spend more time together than we did with our families. At times, he has a crusty and cynical side, and he lets you know it. Almost 20 years of shooting photographs of everything human beings can and will do to one another will make you that way. Seldom does anyone in the newsroom refer to him using his first name. He is "Bonner."

On our 25-minute drive to Union that October morning, Bonner was different. His familiar disposition was not there. Both of us sensed we were working an unusual story – but neither of us realized the national focus that would be directed toward us nine days later.

It was good being paired with Bonner on this story. Both of us grew up in Spartanburg and attended the same high school. The Upstate of South Carolina was familiar turf.

My first job was a carrier route for the *Herald-Journal* when I was 14. For 25 years I worked in marketing jobs and lived out of state. Before I returned in 1992, I worked as a writer for a magazine and lived in Boulder, Colorado.

At the *Herald-Journal* I am a general assignment reporter. In that job, I have covered a wide variety of human experiences. Some of the stories make you laugh, but others break the heart and bring tears. This story of a young mother who said she lost her little boys on a lonely Union County highway would make legions of people weep. It was the fourth tragic story about young children I'd covered in 1994.

In January I had watched as firefighters rescued three unconscious children from a burning apartment building. For weeks, I followed their painful recovery and wrote the stories of them and the brave firefighters who saved them. I confess I treated the two men who saved the little girl and her two brothers as heroes. So did the Augusta Burn Center in Georgia. The little girl stayed there several months, and the hospital had the brave firefighters down for a special award ceremony. Then in the summer, I stood by the grave of a tiny baby who died in the hospital. The parents never returned to claim the little boy. They vanished. He spent 30 days in a Gaffney, South Carolina, morgue waiting for someone who'd have him. When the story ran, family members recognized the parents' names and claimed the little boy's body. In September, I watched as people in a neighborhood north of Spartanburg helped the parents of a missing child search for their 2-year-old boy. He was later found dead, after he'd accidently locked himself in the rear seat of a neighbor's car on a warm day. He had suffocated.

Now, I was facing yet another story about children with the potential for a tragic ending.

"If the number of police officers here has anything to do with finding those babies, they will be found," said Ralph, as he walked up to us in the parking lot. "I've never seen so many police officers in one place in my life."

Ralph was just six weeks from retiring and had spent 34 years covering Union County for the newspaper. Because he knows most of the people who live there, we decided he should stay at the courthouse in case Michael and Alex Smith were found. If an arrest were made, he would be able to move on it quickly. Bonner and I would head out into the county to check the places Susan Smith said she had been the night of October 25.

Before we left, Union County Sheriff Howard Wells called the members of the press into his small courthouse office for a briefing. Four reporters, one newspaper photographer and two television cameramen attended Wells' first press conference.

It was the first time I'd met Howard Wells. He was in his shirt sleeves and wore a bright gold badge on the waistband of his pants. As we entered the reception area, he told us to go in his office and have a seat. There were just enough chairs for the reporters. Our photographers stood behind us.

Wells walked in carrying a black three-ring binder and sat down at his desk. He introduced himself and opened the binder. He never smiled and rarely changed his expression. He kept the notebook open and referred to it several times when questions were asked. Wells began the press conference abruptly, and that's how he ended it. We were in his office about 15 minutes.

"Well, let's go see the intersection where he got in her car first and then follow the route she took," I said to Bonner as we walked back outside.

Two women walked into the parking lot just as we were about to leave. One of them carried a stack of 5x7 color photographs.

"Here are pictures of the boys," one woman said. "Susan had them taken in our studio in August."

The other woman passed out the photographs. There were several different poses, but all of them pictured both Alex and

Michael. For a moment, I stood there looking at the photographs the woman had handed me.

Dear God, I thought. How can the parents stand this? These children are beautiful.

The traffic light where Highway 49 and Peach Orchard Road intersect turned red just before we reached it. As we waited for the light to change, I looked around the intersection to see what was there.

The Bethel United Methodist Church parking lot was directly left of us and Monarch Mill parking lot was to our right. Thick woods were across the street and to the left. The mill was across the street to the right. Both the mill and the company parking lot were surrounded by an eight-foot cyclone fence.

"It all began right here," I said, rather casually. "This seems like a busy place. I wonder why no one saw the man jump in her car?"

It's a pretty drive northeast along Highway 49. Within minutes you clear Union's downtown and enter a beautiful landscape of rolling South Carolina farmland. Near the entrance to John D. Long Lake, Bonner pulled over to the shoulder of the road and stopped.

"This is the spot where he put her out of the car," he said as we got out to look around. "Which of these houses do you think she went to?"

From where we were standing two houses were visible. One was located at the end of a long dirt lane, and the other one was about 100 yards away on the east side of the road. It was the one Susan Smith had chosen.

As we got back into the van, I noticed a man looking through the weeds and bushes along the roadway. When we asked him what he was doing, he said he was looking for anything the police could use to help find the children. He said it was his day off and he volunteered to help in the search.

On the other side of the highway, a large sign marked the entrance to the lake. "Let's take a look, " I suggested as Bonner turned onto the black top road that led to the parking lot. He stopped at the top of the boat ramp and got out to walk around. The dam was just north of where we parked. Two fishermen, seated on small folding stools, watched us as we explored the grassy picnic area.

Large trees grow close to the water's edge on much of the shoreline. On the morning of October 26, the wind was calm. The changing leaves were mirrored on the still water in autumn splendor.

"What a beautiful place," I said as we stood and talked near the water's edge on the ramp. "Let's head back."

"I don't believe her," Bonner said as he pulled the van back onto Highway 49 for the nine-mile drive back to Union.

"Here's what could have happened." And he told his story. "Or this." He told another version.

"Bonner, stop it," I told him. "I have to be objective and I don't want these ideas in my head when I start writing."

He was right. Susan Smith's story made no sense at all.

"Why would a black man on the run want two screaming children in the back seat of the car?" I asked. The question went unanswered.

Our tour of the places where Susan Smith said the crime happened the night before lasted just over an hour. When we returned to the courthouse, we saw Ralph Greer standing in the hallway by the tax collector's office. We told him what we had seen. I asked Ralph if he knew the family and would he call them about our getting an interview with the parents of the missing children.

"Sure, I've known them for years," he said. "I'll give them a call." Moments later, he was talking to Bev Russell, Susan Smith's stepfather.

"The more press they get, the better the chances of finding the boys," Ralph told him. Within minutes Ralph had convinced him. "Okay, they'll be right out there," he said and hung up the telephone.

Ralph drew a map to show us how to reach Bev and Linda Russell's home in Mt. Vernon Estates, eight miles east of Union.

When we arrived there about 20 minutes later, cars filled the driveway and lined both sides of the road in front of the Russell home. There was constant activity, as people arrived and others left. At least 25 people, most of them men, were standing around in small groups talking. The driver of a florist delivery truck walked past carrying two large arrangements of fresh flowers.

Most of the visitors were using a carport entrance to the home, so Bonner and I followed them. Before we reached the door, Bev Russell met us and introduced himself. "I've never experienced anything like this waiting," said Russell as we shook hands. "I've experienced death, but never anything like this. I don't want any bad news either. Susan is sedated and can't talk with you," he continued. "She is asleep, but David will be right out."

Moments later, the door opened and David Smith walked over to where Bonner and I were waiting. It was the first time I had met the 24-year-old father of Michael and Alex Smith. He was still wearing the blue dress shirt and red tie he wore to work at Union's Winn-Dixie Marketplace the night before.

A night without sleep, endless weeping and deep fear for the safety of his children had left a look on the young father's face that caused me to choke back tears as I spoke to him.

"Can we just do this outside?" he asked. "It's really crowded in the house." As he spoke, we walked around the corner to the Russell's back yard, out of sight from the constant flow of people entering and leaving.

"I'm sorry about this, David," I said to him. "Thank you for talking to me. Getting the story to the media will help."

Toys that belonged to his two children were scattered about the screened porch behind him.

> "Everywhere I look, I see their play toys and pictures," David told me in a soft voice. "They are both wonderful children. I don't know how else to put it. I can't imagine life without them."

David is assistant manager at the large grocery store where he works. He said he learned his estranged wife had been car-jacked shortly after 9 p.m. the previous night. The sheriff's officers called him and told him to come to Shirley McCloud's house on Highway 49. The tears started again as he spoke.

> "I thought I was going to go out of my mind as I drove out there," the young father said. "I'd never experienced that kind of fear. I didn't know how to react."

As David spoke, I could hear the sound of Bonner's camera capturing the distraught face of a young father, desperate for help.

David Smith and I talked for about 30 minutes. His interview was the best thing we had gotten in several hours of reporting. In fact, it was the only thing other than what Wells had told us in his office.

We shook hands and I told David goodbye. I watched, with a lump in my throat, as he turned and walked into the house.

On the way to Bonner's van, one of the men standing in the driveway spoke to us. It was Walt Garner, the father of Donna Garner – Susan Smith's friend since the girls were toddlers. Garner and his wife had kept Alex and Michael at their home on

Monday night while Susan attended night classes at the Union campus of the University of South Carolina. I asked him if he would talk with me briefly and he said he would.

"We've been out all night looking for Susan's car," Garner said. "We came in to get something to eat, and then we're going out again."

Union County is a sparsely settled area of South Carolina. Only 33,000 people live in the entire county. The area is known for its dense forests and wood production. Walt Garner and his friends had been driving the countless miles of side roads and fire lanes where someone could hide a 1990 Mazda Protegé.

> "I held those babies in my lap Monday night," Garner said as he struggled to speak. "I've known Susan since she was a child. These children are close to me."

I thanked Walt Garner for his time, wished him the best and started to the van. But just as I was about to turn, Susan and David Smith walked out of the carport with Linda Russell, Susan's mother. The three of them got into David's beige Honda and drove away.

Sheriff Howard Wells had called. He wanted to interview both David and Susan again. When we arrived back at the court-house later that morning, David's Honda was parked along the curb by a "No Parking" sign outside the sheriff's office. It stayed there until late Wednesday afternoon. Police sources told us the couple had been questioned all day, in separate rooms.

It was lunchtime when Bonner and I returned to town. Earlier that morning we had spotted O'Dell's, a cafe that adver-tised "home-style" cooking. That's where Bonner stopped the van for lunch. The intersection where Susan said the man jumped in her car is less than a block away. It's clearly visible from the cafe.

"Y'all must be reporters," said the woman behind the counter, as she dished up generous portions of black-eyed peas, turnip greens, meatloaf and cornbread. "I guess we will be seeing a lot of you for awhile."

I followed Bonner to a table near the front of the restaurant.

"Bonner, you may be right." I told him, as we ate. "This story is full of holes. The car can't just vanish."

"There's something about that lake that bothers me," he said.

As we ate, the news that began filtering out to police departments all over the nation the night before continued. No more than 30 minutes after officers arrived at Shirley McCloud's house Tuesday night, computer terminals in police stations all over the United States carried the news from Union. Police dispatchers throughout the Carolinas announced the first BOLO (Be On The Lookout) – the police term for a car or person being sought by officers. The announcement continued 24 hours a day, as police all over the United States searched for a black man driving a burgundy Mazda with two white children in the back seat.

After we finished lunch, we decided to drive back to the lake. On the way, we passed several television satellite trucks headed toward Union. As we topped the hill near Shirley McCloud's house, we could see the entrance to the lake was blocked by an orange barricade.

"I'll bet they're searching the lake," Bonner said as he stopped the van on the shoulder of the highway.

"Yes, and we need photographs, if they are," I replied.

For a moment, we discussed bushwhacking our way through

tall weeds and brush so we could climb to the top of the dam and observe. It would be a great spot to photograph the diving operation. Then I spotted a house high on a bluff overlooking the lake. I liked the idea of walking through the woods behind the house to reach the lake better, because I was pretty certain there was an abundant snake population in the tall weeds behind the dam.

"Yeah, several news people have been here already," the man who owned the house told us. "It's an easy walk to the lake back there."

By the time we reached a point where we had full view of the lake, the divers were gone.

"We've been hearing helicopters out here all morning," the man told us. "They must be landing over at the other entrance."

Bonner and I looked at one another. "Where's the other entrance?" I asked.

The road off Highway 9 that leads to the south side of the lake was narrow and winding. I thought we would never get to the parking area. Two television news teams had arrived at the parking lot ahead of Bonner and me. WIS-TV in Columbia had gotten there in time to get a cameraman on board the South Carolina Law Enforcement Division helicopter that circled overhead.

When the helicopter landed, Sheriff Wells confirmed divers had searched the lake. The sheriff said he and SLED officers had been on an aerial search of the woods around the lake but had seen nothing unusual.

Traffic was slow as we drove back into town along Union's Main Street. Near the courthouse it crawled. Television satellite trucks and curious onlookers clogged the streets. When Bonner and I left a few hours earlier, there were three satellite trucks parked near the courthouse. Now, they were beginning to fill both sides of the street for a city block.

By the following day, all the major television networks had crews on the scene. There were 15 satellite trucks with their large dishes pointed toward the southwestern skies. Reporters from newspapers all along the east coast were there as well.

It seemed odd to see the national press working alongside the local reporters. The well-known correspondents were aggressive and made things move faster. I determined the first day they arrived in town that I would not allow them to outpace me and I don't think they did. On several occasions, I saw reporters from the networks carrying our newspaper around. I was proudest when I'd catch one of them reading what I had written. From the tiny *Union Daily Times*, the state's smallest daily newspaper, to the largest news organizations in the country, the media were well represented – including WBCU, the local radio station. Just like the television networks, they broadcast every news conference live to their Union County listeners.

"Well, there's nothing new here," said Ralph, as we approached him in the parking lot. "The sheriff said he'll hold a briefing later this afternoon."

In the meantime, we waited. Ralph and I compared notes on what we had for the next day's newspaper. I decided to walk along Main Street and get reactions from shop owners and people I met on the street.

Union residents gathered along the sidewalk and watched as an army of local, state and federal officers came and went from the command center. The area was also the center of activity for reporters because that's where news conferences were held. A large bank of microphones was always in place, just inside the gate. Sometimes, the onlookers would drift in to mingle with reporters.

Kevin Kingsmore, a 23-year-old local graphic artist, was among those in the crowd when Bonner and I returned. He had worked all morning to design a flier that volunteers would begin handing out all over the Upstate later in the day.

"About 200 people will be meeting later today to get orga-
nized," Kingsmore said. "We're going to post these all over the
state." Twenty-seven-year-old Wendy Fowler took a stack of
fliers from Kingsmore. "I've been out looking all afternoon,"
she said. "I'm doing everything I can. I've prayed for these children all morning."

Kingsmore's fliers were posted all over South Carolina and
throughout the South. By the middle of the week the fliers were
seen as far away as Illinois.

Word about the missing children was passed on by truckers.
Citizen Band radios in the big rigs broadcast the sad news about
the boys' disappearance all day Wednesday.

Late in the afternoon a trucker on Interstate 85 near
Anderson, South Carolina, reported a car matching the description of Susan Smith's Mazda. State troopers and a helicopter
rushed to the area, but found no sign of the car.

By the end of the day, The National Center for Missing and
Exploited Children was notified by authorities. Copies of the
same photos I had received earlier were sent to their Maryland
headquarters by overnight delivery.

The following day a poster was created and distributed
through CompuServe and broadcast by facsimile to 45 state
clearinghouses and 1,600 law enforcement agencies across the
nation.

Throughout the afternoon, I spoke frequently by telephone
from Bonner's van with *Herald-Journal* city desk editors. As
the 4 p.m. budget meeting for the next day's newspaper grew
nearer, city editor Brad Rogers and assistant city editor Diane
Norman pressed me for any new information I may have gathered. There was none.

This afternoon ritual of a budget meeting is the time when
editors decide how the news stories will be played the following

morning. We knew we were page one, but the editors wanted something fresh, not a rehash of information we had printed in the first story.

When the news conference ended, I was ready to return to the newsroom in Spartanburg. It was a 30-mile drive and I wanted to write my story for the next day's newspaper so I could go home. But David and Susan Smith were still in the sheriff's office, and Bonner saw the opportunity for more photographs when they left.

The longer we waited, the more nervous I became about my deadline. I knew I was writing the lead story for Thursday's newspaper and I wanted all the time I could get in front of my computer terminal.

But just after 6:30 p.m. Bonner was rewarded for his patience. Susan and David Smith came out the side entrance to the courthouse and walked to their car, and he was the only photographer around at the time. One of the photographs he shot while Susan walked to the car appeared on the front page of the *Herald-Journal* the following morning – and on the cover of *Time* magazine the following week.

As soon as Bonner shot the photo, we headed for the newsroom.

"Ralph has already sent his story," Diane Norman said as I walked to my desk. "We're waiting for yours."

The newsroom is always a busy, and sometimes tense, place as deadline nears each night. The voices from two communications scanners rarely stop putting out police, fire and Emergency Medical Service calls. Tonight, they were also putting out a BOLO for Susan Smith's burgundy Mazda. The tension was different from anything I'd felt before in this familiar place.

"We've got the news stuff," Diane said. "You're writing a sidebar on color and atmosphere down there."

I wrote a story describing how people in Union County reacted to Alex and Michael's abduction. It was a mood piece that showed the sad feelings people expressed to me throughout the day – and it showed their determination to help find two Union County toddlers.

I was almost finished writing the story when Carmela walked in the newsroom with my dinner.

"I thought you would be hungry."

And I was. I had not thought about eating, but I was suddenly starving. Before I ate, I finished my story and sent it on to the city desk for edit. Carmela and I talked about what I'd experienced that day, while Diane read my story. It was our first conversation since early that morning. Carmela was unable to hide the empathy she felt for the young mother who'd lost her two children. She continued to ask me questions about what I'd seen during the day and say how horrible it would be to have that happen.

"This looks fine," Diane told me. "We'll package it on A-1 with Ralph's story."

Just after 9:30 p.m. I realized I was exhausted, and I was ready to go home. But I was bothered that I had not interviewed Susan Smith about her story. So I decided to try again. "I'll be ready to leave after I make this call," I said to Carmela as I dialed the telephone.

"May I speak to Susan Smith?" I asked.

"This is Susan," the young woman answered. My heart almost jumped out of my chest, but I did not want her to detect any tension in my voice.

"Susan, would it be all right if I ask you a few brief questions? I know it must be difficult for you."

"Yes, I'll answer a few questions for you."

I did not want to be overbearing, but yet I knew this might be the only chance I'd have to speak with her. She was polite and cordial. And I expressed how sorry I was about the man taking her children.

Susan Smith's willingness to talk had caught me off-guard. As we spoke, I tried to signal Diane to let her know who I had on the telephone, while taking notes at the same time. It was more difficult because I was using a telephone in the work station next to my own. I couldn't find a reporter's notebook, so I was taking notes on pieces of paper from the wastebasket.

Finally, Carmela saw my dilemma and got my editor's attention. When Diane walked over, I started phrasing questions so she would know who was on the telephone with me. Diane ran to the copy desk and told them the front page was about to change. Meanwhile, Susan continued to tell me her strange story.

> "I stood in the middle of the road and screamed 'I love y'all' as he drove away with my children," Susan told me. "I was on the way to a friend's house and had to stop for the red light," she continued. "The door opened and this man just got in. I was looking out the window on my side of the car and didn't see him coming. He was out of breath, like he had been running."

"What did he say to you, Susan?" I asked her, pushing on with the questions.

> "He had a gun and he told me to drive or he would kill me," she replied. "The boys started crying after he got in the car. Michael asked, 'Who is this man, Mommy?' I begged him to let me keep my children," Susan continued. "He told me, 'I don't have time. I'll take care of them.' "

What surprised me was that Susan never broke down. She never sounded as though she was crying even once during the 15-minute conversation. I commended her for holding up so well under such trying circumstances. I wondered how a woman whose two children were kidnapped 24 hours earlier could be so composed.

Before we hung up, I told Susan I would like to speak with her further. She said I could meet her at the Russell's at 9 a.m. the following morning.

"Start writing," Diane said. We were getting very close to deadline by now. To speed things along, I told her to type and I would dictate the story. Diane is a fast typist and would get ahead of my dictation as I stood over her shoulder and composed copy. I hate dictating a story, but under the circumstances, we'd never have made deadline if I had not done it at that time.

In 15 minutes, the story was done. It was the lead story in Thursday's newspaper. The *Herald-Journal* was the only newspaper in the nation that had an interview with Susan or this version of her story.

By 10:30 p.m. my story was edited and at the copy desk. But I wanted to see the proofs of Thursday morning's front page before I left for home. While we waited Diane and I watched the 11 p.m. news on television.

Suddenly, the police scanners caught our attention. A dispatcher was sending Spartanburg County Sheriff's officers to a dirt road in the Springfield neighborhood in the northern part of Spartanburg County. A motorist had seen a burgundy car with the rear window shot out parked on the side of the road. Toys and children's clothing were scattered all around it.

I jumped up, grabbed a walkie-talkie and headed for the door. Photographer Matthew Fortner had heard the call go out over the photo lab scanner. We met as we both started for the stairs at the rear of the newsroom.

"Do you know where the road is?" Matthew asked me as he drove out of the employee parking lot. "Yes," I replied. "Just head up the Asheville Highway."

As we drove, Diane and I talked by radio.

"Radio back as soon as you know something," she said.

My heart pounded.

"Maybe this is over," I said to Matthew. "But where are the kids? Nothing was said about them."

It was a fast trip to Springfield Crossing. We had not seen any police cars en route, so I was beginning to think it was probably a false alarm.

"If this was the real thing, they would have all the cops in the county up here," I said as we approached the dirt road where the car was parked. It was a 4-door burgundy car, but this one was a Toyota, not a Mazda. The rear window of the car appeared to have been blown out.

After Matthew stopped behind the car, I realized we were in a pretty desolate area. It was very dark and we were the only people I saw. I suggested to Matthew that we should not stick around. Just as we started to leave, another car drove up with two men in it. They told us they lived nearby and they had called the police after they heard gunshots. One of them said he thought it must have been some kind of domestic dispute. I was relieved when Matthew pulled away. We never heard anything further about the incident.

It was almost midnight when we got back to the newsroom. First edition "proofs" were spread out on a table. Copy editors were giving Thursday's newspaper a final check for errors.

In a few hours, readers would be pouring over the second of more than 60 stories we reported about Susan Smith and the disappearance of her two children. I looked at the proof and walked slowly out of the newsroom to my car. It was the first time that day I'd had allowed my personal feelings to surface. After my visit with David 12 hours earlier and my telephone conversation with Susan, I wondered how these young parents would hold up. This was a sad story.

I drove home just after 1 a.m., and collapsed in bed for a night of restless sleep.

DAY II

October 27, 1994

The morning dawned clear and crisp. The temperature was in the 40s but the National Weather Service was calling for a high of 62 degrees by mid-afternoon. Upstate South Carolina was in for another gorgeous fall day.

When I awoke that Thursday morning, my first thought was about the interview I had scheduled with Susan Smith. Even though I had only about three hours sleep, I was not tired. I pulled on my bathrobe and headed for the front yard to bring in the morning newspaper.

The proof I'd seen the night before had been in black and white and it did not include photos. But the *Herald-Journal* second edition I held in my hand was in full-color, including the photograph of 3-year-old Michael and his 14-month-old brother, Alex. It was the first of many times their photo appeared in our newspapers during the search for them.

"Well, there they are," I said to Carmela as I placed the open paper on the dining room table. Before me was the headline that would later be repeated in national magazines and in newspapers around the world.

"A mother's frantic call: 'I love y'all' "

Carmela took the paper in her hand and read the story she had seen me writing the previous night. "The boys are beautiful," she said with her voice breaking. "How could she let him drive away with them in the car and not put up a fight?"

It was a question that echoed all over the country that morning, and one I planned to ask Susan Smith about in two hours.

This was the second day Susan Smith had been on our front page. But this morning her story was more than a brief. It filled more than half the front page and continued with a full page of stories and more photographs inside.

A second story I had written about how the people of Union County were helping with the search for the children was at the top of the inside page. A story by police beat reporter Reggie Fields gave tips on how to prevent a carjacking.

Just after 7:30 a.m. Carmela and I left for her office. "Good luck today," she said as she got out of the car. "I won't expect you home for dinner."

That was a good plan. During the search for Alex and Michael Smith, I rarely made it home before 11 p.m. Most nights, I ate dinner at my desk while I wrote the next day's story for the newspaper. During the 9-day search, I had dinner at home twice.

Neither Bonner nor I were going to the office before we left town, so we planned to meet at the Union County Courthouse at 8:30 a.m. As I drove east of Spartanburg along Highway 176, I planned what I would ask Susan. And like many people who live in Spartanburg County, I listened to WSPA-AM's morning radio personality and friend, Bill Drake. At 8 a.m., Bill switched to CBS News in New York. Their lead story was about a young mother whose children were taken from her when she was carjacked in Union, South Carolina.

Susan Smith's voice was speaking on my radio.

She was telling the story of the black man who took her children.

A large crowd of reporters were already milling about in the parking lot by the sheriff's office when I arrived. I spotted Bonner standing by the CNN satellite truck. He was chatting with several photographers I did not know and Cliff LaBlanc, a writer for *The State* newspaper in Columbia, South Carolina.

"Good morning," said Bonner, without mentioning our 9 a.m. appointment. "We're back at it for another day."

Cliff turned and extended his right hand to shake mine. In his other hand, he held a copy of Thursday morning's *Herald-Journal*.

"Nice job on getting the interview with Susan," Cliff said. "You beat everybody in the state of South Carolina on that one."

It was a sincere compliment from an outstanding journalist and respected colleague. I appreciated Cliff's kind remarks, but I did not tell him, or anyone else, where Bonner and I were going when we left in his van.

The scene at the Russell's house was the same as the day before. Cars lined both sides of the street and there was constant activity as people entered and left the house.

We arrived right on time at 9 a.m. Susan's stepfather, Bev Russell, met us at the door. "Come in," said Russell, cordially. "They'll be out in just a minute."

As he spoke, Russell placed a chair by a small sofa and indicated that is where I should sit. Bonner was making last minute checks with his cameras. While we waited, I complimented Russell on his attractive home. He told us about the remodeling he had done in the house. Cut flower arrangements and potted plants were everywhere. So was food. It reminded me of when there's been a death and friends bring in food for the grieving family.

While we were talking, David and Susan Smith entered the room. It was the first time I had been that close to Susan. She was carrying a box of tissue and both of them appeared to have been crying. They still were. Susan never looked me directly in the eyes. Not even once. Her shoulder-length hair fell loosely around her face. The day before her hair had been pulled back and tied with a bow.

David was different. His eyes were red, and he appeared distraught, but he looked directly at me when he spoke. He was unable to hide his grief. Both of them looked as though they had just stepped out of the shower and dressed. David wore a green sweater and jeans and Susan wore a light pink pullover top with khaki pants.

"We almost called and told you not to come," said Russell as David and Susan took their seats. "We have decided to stop the interviews for awhile, but since Susan had told you she would do this one, we decided to let you come on."

As I spoke with Susan, Russell walked to a chair behind me and sat down. He stayed with us throughout the interview. It made me a little nervous because it felt like he was there to monitor our conversation.

"I'm very sorry about this, Susan," I said as we started talking. "Being the father of two children, I have some idea of how much it must hurt." I could hear Bonner's cameras operating without let up. I knew he was thinking the same thing I was: "If this is to be the last interview for awhile, then let's get everything we can."

It was a wise choice for him. Like the photographs he had taken the day before, these would end up in national magazines.

As Susan spoke she seemed to lose some of her composure and stopped a couple of times and dabbed at her eyes with a tissue. But, again, I was amazed how well she was handling herself.

"All I can do now is trust in the Lord and my family," Susan said. "I keep trying not to lose hope, but the more time passes, I get scared."

The couple had separated in August, two months earlier, and David had moved out of their house on Toney Road. But as Susan spoke, the 24-year-old father reached over and took her hand.

"If they are lying somewhere dead, I want them home," Susan Smith told me. "Oh God, I can't bear to think of that." As she finished the statement, Susan looked down at the floor. When she did, David spoke. "If something has happened to them, I want to know that too, but I can't bear to think of them dead."

"Not knowing for sure what happened to them makes so many things go through your mind," Susan added. "I pray somebody may find them. I can't put in words how I feel. My heart is in a thousand pieces."

Then Susan told the story again about how the black man she had described to police officers had taken her children. She said she ran down the middle of the road yelling, "Somebody's got my children," after he drove away.

David spoke again: "Every time the phone rings, I cringe because I don't know what news we'll hear. I still have a lot of hope they are out there somewhere okay. I could not go on if I lose hope. This all seems unbelievable."

As I was finishing my interview, Susan Smith expressed optimism that her children would be found alive.

"I have a lot of hope," she said to me. "I can't imagine life without my children."

Susan Smith continued to speak about the questions officers had asked her.

> "I told them I would never hurt my children. I've been heartbroken by this. I hope for the best and try to be prepared for the worst."

Looking back, I've wondered if her cries for help really echoed through the woods on that dark and lonely stretch of Highway 49 the night of October 25. Or did she walk calmly along the road to Shirley McCloud's house, fake hysteria, and tell her phony carjacking story for the first time? And why did she sometimes slip into the past tense when talking about her children?

"The woman kept telling me, 'Everything will be okay,' " Susan said. "She put her arms around me and held me."

I was beginning to sense Susan wanted to end the interview because she seemed a little slower in answering questions. Since she had been so cooperative with me, I was hoping that I could get her to talk with me at a later date, regardless of what Bev Russell had told me. I decided to take what I had and leave.

We thanked David and Susan for their time, and Bev Russell showed us to the door.

"I don't know, maybe she is telling the truth," said Bonner as we walked toward the van. "But the whole thing still doesn't make sense."

On the ride back into town Bonner went through the story again, as it had been told to us. I wanted to believe Susan Smith because I was having difficulty accepting the idea that a mother may have killed her children.

We arrived back in town shortly after 10 a.m. I don't think either of us were prepared for the sight we saw. Yellow ribbons were being attached to the front doors of every business along

Main Street. Union High School senior Daniel Glenn was tying yellow ribbons to each of the 32 holly trees that line the street.

"I volunteered for this," Glenn said. "I hope this is sending a message, letting everybody know how serious a problem it is. And I hope I'm doing my part."

The people of Union were preparing to welcome Alex and Michael home.

"I've never experienced anything like this. I feel like they are my own," said Pat Gibson as she tied a ribbon on her door. "I'm keeping this up until the children come home."

By early afternoon, almost every car you saw had a yellow ribbon attached to its antenna.

A news briefing had taken place early that morning, but now things were quiet. So we headed to Just Lunch, a little German restaurant on Gadberry Street. It was the first of several meals we would have there. Bonner knew the owner from a previous assignment he'd worked. The locals at the restaurant gave us looks that said, "We know you are visitors." I guess our *Herald-Journal* identification badges, beepers and the cameras hanging around Bonner's shoulders made it obvious.

Before we left to walk downtown I took a stroll around the courthouse, inside and outside. I spotted a telephone company installer working the lines leading into the building.

"We're adding telephone lines," the man said. "They need them to handle the calls coming in."

Earlier, Margaret Frierson with The Adam Walsh Foundation in Columbia, South Carolina, had told us the organization was getting the message out to its chapters all over the United States.

"We tend to get a lot of calls where there are children involved," she told reporters. "Time is our biggest problem and we have to be able to respond quickly." Frierson went on to say the television show "America's Most Wanted" was on "standby" to help. John Walsh, the television show's host, is the father of

Adam Walsh, a little boy who disappeared several years ago in Florida. In two days a thousand calls offering tips that might help find Alex and Michael were received at the command center in Union.

Divers went back to the lake on Thursday, but found no trace of the car. Howard Wells told the media: "I'm confident the car is not in the lake. We did it to rule out any evidence that we might have overlooked there."

Wells would not comment about whether David and Susan had taken lie detector tests, but sources told one of our reporters both took tests on Thursday. The sources told us David passed his test but Susan did not. Hers was declared inconclusive.

A short time after Bonner and I had returned to the courthouse from lunch, I overheard a conversation between two women I did not know.

"I heard David and Susan haven't lived together for a couple of months and they are getting a divorce," one of them said.

"I'll see you a little later," I said to Bonner as I headed inside the courthouse to find the Clerk of Courts office. I knew if they had filed for divorce, I could learn a lot about the Smiths' private life by reading the filing papers.

"I'll bet you are looking for the same thing I am," said *Charlotte Observer* reporter Bruce Henderson as I walked into the office. "The Clerk of Courts has gone to speak with the judge to see if she can release copies of the divorce papers."

A few minutes later Clerk of Court June Miller walked in.

"Okay, here you are," she said. "That will be $10."

I had only $6 left after lunch but I had to have those papers.

"I can spot you $4," Bruce said. "Make two copies, please."

I was grateful to Bruce for helping me out, but it was at least two weeks after the event was over before I remembered to pay him.

The following morning I reported for the first time that Susan Smith was asking for a divorce on grounds of adultery.

Soon after I returned to the press area from the Clerk of Court's Office, David Smith showed up to speak on nationwide television. He first pleaded for the return of his children and then answered a few brief questions. It was the first of several times he would go before the television cameras during the search to plead for the safe return of his little boys. He refused to answer questions about his pending divorce, although he had not lived in the same house with Susan and the boys since August.

> "I plead with the man to return our children safe and sound," David said. "It gets harder as time goes by to deal with this."

David Smith ended his tearful statement on national television by giving whoever kidnapped his children this advice:

> "Alex needs a bottle before he goes to bed at night."

Gary Henderson

DAYS III, IV, V

October 28 - 30, 1994

On Friday, *Herald-Journal* writer Suellen Dean joined Ralph Greer to cover the events in Union. Lou Parris, who was filling in as city editor that day, asked if I could work the telephones.

"Just start making calls down there," Lou said. "Let's see what we can find."

I knew what Lou wanted . . . work the sources we had developed and try to find something new to write about.

With law enforcement officials I learned nothing new. But a call to a woman named Judy Cathcart in Buffalo, a textile-mill village near Union, yielded nuggets of gold. I learned she was the woman who cared for Alex and Michael each day while their mother worked as a secretary at Conso Products, the largest employer in Union County.

Susan had mentioned her name in our first conversation on the telephone. She said she had picked up the boys from Cathcart's home late on the afternoon of October 25. It seemed unimportant at the time, but I decided to call her anyway.

At first, Cathcart appeared concerned I had gotten her name, but she continued to talk.

"The first morning was the toughest," Cathcart told me. "After their parents dropped the other children off, I tried to explain why Alex and Michael were not here."

As the woman spoke, I could hear Alex and Michael's friends playing in the background. Cathcart went on with her story.

"The children asked if we could pray for Alex and Michael," she said, her voice choking with emotion. "I asked if they wanted to hold hands, but they said no. They wanted to kneel by the sofa."

Cathcart said there is nothing sweeter – or sadder – than when little children pray for their playmates. She said a five year old boy prayed this way:

> "Help this man bring Michael and Alexander back
> to play with us."

Cathcart said she told the children things they could do to be safe, one of which was to always stay with their mommies. But one of the children in her care gave the woman this grim reminder:

> "Michael and Alex were with their mommy when
> something happened to them," the little boy said.

On Thursday, Judy Cathcart and the children hung two yellow ribbons around a big tree in front of her home.

The search by officers and volunteers intensified and spread into North Carolina. During most of Friday, 200 people combed the Uwharrie National Forest in Rowan, Davidson, Stanly and Montgomery Counties. A deer hunter had reported he heard a child's cries in the woods.

In Orange County, North Carolina, a trucker spotted a car

matching the description of Susan Smith's Mazda on Interstate 85.

Late in the day, state and local authorities searched a wooded area near Union High School. Someone said a man matching the description of the man Susan said took her children was seen entering the woods.

Alex and Michael had vanished. So had the black man driving Susan Smith's burgundy Mazda. At a 5 p.m. news conference, Sheriff Howard Wells said he had not ruled out any suspects, including the boys' parents. He also said investigators had found some discrepancies in Susan Smith's statements, but he would not elaborate.

The first few days of the search for Alex and Michael Smith had been long and tiring. Emotions were tattered. I needed a break but I felt uncomfortable taking a weekend off. But our family had planned a trip to Charleston to visit our son Marc and our daughter-in-law Kelli. Marc had taken a job with Charleston County Emergency Medical Services in September. It was to be our first visit with them since they had moved from Spartanburg.

After the week I'd had in Union, I needed to see my family together. Even though our daughter Heather is 19 and Marc is 24, I could still remember the time they were the ages of the two missing children. I thought about those early days of their lives often during that week.

Yes, I needed to have both of them near me, if for only a weekend.

On Saturday while I was in Charleston three other reporters covered the story for the *Herald-Journal*.

Our photographers had rotated in and out of Union, but Bonner stayed there the longest. Most of them were now staying in town on 24-hour shifts, going occasionally to a motel room the newspaper had rented for a nap. Exclusive photographs and stories the *Herald-Journal* had been able to get in the early stages of the story had forced other media to be more aggressive in their coverage.

Bonner was scheduled to be off for six days, with the end of his schedule on Thursday. When he came home from playing in a golf tournament on Friday, he called photo editor Bryan Stiles and requested his time off be canceled so he could be reassigned to Union. On Saturday night he watched movies in the hallway outside the sheriff's office with NBC's "Dateline" crew on a television they "borrowed" from a local motel. Bonner said his desire to be on the story was almost uncontrollable. It was a feeling I had often in Charleston that same weekend.

On Saturday morning we ate breakfast at Billy's Back Home in Mt. Pleasant, South Carolina, near Charleston. CNN "Headline News" played on a large-screen television. When the news cycle started over on the hour, the first story was about how Susan Smith had failed a lie detector test. Seeds of doubt were sprouting.

While it was good to be with my family, my thoughts often drifted back to the events going on in Union. I called the newsroom every few hours during the two days we were in Charleston. What I was hearing on television was not enough.

On Saturday night Union gathered for a candlelight prayer vigil to remember Alex and Michael. It seemed the entire city was searching and praying they would be returned unharmed.

Sunday was warm and humid in Charleston. We got up early and headed to the Sea Biscuit on the Isle of Palms for breakfast. While we waited outside for a table, I bought a *Charleston Post and Courier* newspaper and leaned against the car to read. But what I really wanted was a copy of the *Herald-Journal.* I wanted to see what my colleagues had written.

We arrived back in Spartanburg early Sunday evening. As soon as I had unloaded the car, I headed straight for the newsroom. I learned volunteers had combed sections of Union County on horseback looking for the children. Divers had once again searched John D. Long Lake.

For the people of Union County, the search for Alex and Michael was beginning to feel personal. Two of their little boys were missing.

Gary Henderson

DAY VI

October 31, 1994

On Monday, police beat reporter Reggie Fields and I were sent to Union. We decided he would concentrate on the police search and I would get out in the community and look for a color sidebar story.

It was Halloween and a week to the day since Alex and Michael had disappeared.

Cool temperatures gave the day a real feeling of autumn as hundreds of costumed children went to each of the businesses on Main Street. For the first time in days, Union smiled – if only for a couple of hours.

"These children have to go on. They can't continue to be sad," said Mamie McBeth, a retired schoolteacher who taught for 30 years. "They have to feel like children, but they just have to be more careful."

McBeth, now with the Union County Schools' Parents Resource Center on Main Street, recognized many of the children. The ones she knew received more than a candy treat. They got a warm greeting and a tight hug.

"We are still praying and thinking about the little children,

37

but at the same time, we have to get on with our lives," she told me.

From the north end of Main Street to the courthouse on the south end, children played trick or treat. They were just being kids. The gathered media loved it. It seemed to be a relief from what we had covered for the past seven days.

CBS News correspondent Elizabeth Kaledin finished a report for the network's Seattle affiliate. She and the rest of the crew immediately began handing out more Reese's Peanut Butter Cups. Engineers had taped a large sign to the side of the CBS truck: "Trick or Treaters welcome."

"The people of Union have been wonderful," Kaledin said. "They brought in chicken and biscuits for lunch today. It was delicious. We are paying back their hospitality."

As dusk fell, the children left Main Street and the reporters returned to the task at hand. Television lights lit small areas all around the courthouse lawn and beside the satellite trucks, as television crews began feeding live broadcasts back to their stations in distant cities.

Monday was the slowest day of the investigation. Officers told us they were regrouping and looking for new ways to pursue the investigation.

Like reporters, the citizens of Union were beginning to doubt Susan's story.

"It's a hoax," said Howard Free. "It's just a hoax. I think the mother knows something about it all and I think that's the way about 95 percent of the people down here think."

While others agreed, they didn't think Susan would hurt her little boys.

"I don't think the mother hurt those babies, but she knows more than she is telling," Roberta Gathing said. "I want to believe her, but I've been reading between the lines and it doesn't add up."

Mitch Sinclair, the man Susan said she was on the way to visit the night the boys were kidnapped, told the television show "A Current Affair" that the lie detector test he took did not go well.

Sinclair's younger brother, 17-year-old Patrick Sinclair, told reporters, "I think the kids are hidden somewhere, but my brother didn't do it. If he did, then that's some crazy stuff."

Mitch Sinclair would not comment about his statements when a *Herald-Journal* reporter reached him at Bev Russell's home.

After Sheriff Wells' final press briefing of the day, I headed back up Highway 176 to the newsroom in Spartanburg. There are places along that road where the Blue Ridge Mountains of North Carolina can be seen clearly. I drank in the sight of the blue-colored hills, the changing autumn leaves and the orange glow in the Western Carolina sky. As I drove, I thought about Susan Smith and her children, and I wondered how anything so bad could have happened in a place like Union.

Gary Henderson

DAY VII

November 1, 1994

On Tuesday, Reggie Fields, Janet Spencer from our Gaffney bureau and I returned to Union. They followed the sheriff's investigation. I spent the day trying to learn anything I could by talking to people and going back over my notes of earlier days of the investigation. It was the slowest day of the search for the media.

The highlight of the day was when sheriff's officers announced they had ruled out Mitch Sinclair as a suspect in the abduction. Many people had suspected he was involved because Susan told officers she was on the way to Sinclair's house when she was carjacked and her children were abducted. It was later learned he was not at home and knew nothing about Susan Smith's plan to visit with him.

The morning had gone slowly. No new information was being released by the sheriff's department or any other investigative agency.

"We are going for barbecue," said Bonner as I caught up with him crossing the street. "Come on, go with us. *The New York Times* crew is all going."

It sounded good. The *Herald-Journal* is owned by *The New York Times* Company, but we rarely see their staff members and writers. Rick Bragg, one of my favorite newspaper writers anywhere, was there and I was anxious to meet him. Bragg, an Alabama native, works out of the company's Atlanta office.

"Every town in America ought to have a restaurant like this," said Rick as he skillfully worked on a plate of barbecue pork and assorted country-style vegetables.

With six journalists seated at one table, the conversation never varied far from shoptalk. But much of my conversation with Rick was about an award-winning piece he wrote for his "mama" a few years ago on Mother's Day. It was a sensitive and wonderful piece of writing. I knew why *The New York Times* sent him to Union.

After we returned to the courthouse from lunch, we heard divers were searching a canal in the mill town of Lockhart, just a few miles from John D. Long Lake. When I got there a large group of people had gathered along the highway to watch the divers. Another search was under way in some woods a few miles away in Chester County. A large contingent of press had followed the officers out of town. Bonner and I believed this search and possibly others may have been conducted to give the investigators at the courthouse a little room to operate unnoticed.

Later that afternoon I ventured out to the Russell's home once again. Cars still jammed the street and driveway. An "Inside Edition" satellite truck was parked by the driveway. The television show's co-anchor, Madeline McFadden, was leaning against her rented Toyota sedan.

"If something doesn't break, I guess we are leaving," she said. "I've been right here all day."

We chatted a little longer and I drove back into Union so I could be there for Sheriff Wells' 5:30 p.m. news conference.

As reporters pushed harder for answers, the level of tension between Wells and the media seemed to increase. Once, when I asked a follow-up to another reporter's question, Wells turned and declined to answer. I'll always remember the scowl on his face when he looked at me. The question was so insignificant I do not remember what it was.

Later, I learned my sister, Myra Horne, who lives in Fort Smith, Arkansas saw the exchange on CNN.

As soon as the news conference ended, I headed back to the newsroom.

When I reached town, I detoured to the Spartanburg High School gymnasium. It was election day and I wanted to vote.

It was the only day that I went to Union and did not write a story for the next day's newspaper.

Gary Henderson

DAY VIII

November 2, 1994

By Wednesday the long hours and emotional strain were beginning to show on the faces of everyone involved with covering this story. While I wanted to go back to Union, I was relieved when city editor Brad Rogers said two other reporters would go.

"You need a break, Gary," Brad said. "I'll probably have to send you down there over the weekend."

I hated to admit it, but I knew he was right. Just being on the scene of any story for eight to ten hours, plus the writing time in the newsroom can be exhausting. This story was getting more difficult by the day because we were getting little new information to write about, forcing us to look even harder for information. There were also the daily shifts of emotions to deal with. When reports surfaced that Susan's car had been seen, my spirits would be lifted. The sheriff's announcements that they were unfounded made them crash.

But even though I did not go to Union, I still worked on the story.

Because David and Susan were no longer granting interviews, Margaret Gregory came on as the family spokeswoman. Gregory, the official spokesperson for the Richland County Sheriff's Office in Columbia, is married to one of Susan's cousins. While she would not get the media award as a great diplomat, she did keep the press away from them. For several days, they were not seen by members of the media. That decision disturbed one visitor to Union who had arrived to help.

Marc Klaas, the father of a Petaluma, California girl who had been murdered a year earlier, spent four days in Union and was among those blocked from seeing David and Susan. He said he tried every day to speak with them, but Gregory turned him away.

Klaas, now a journalist with the television show "American Journal," was the father of Polly Klaas, who had been abducted about a year earlier while she was entertaining friends at a slumber party. Her body was found two months later about 50 miles from her home – stuffed under a stack of plywood.

On Wednesday, the day after Klaas left, I located him in his hotel room in Los Angeles. "I tried to make it clear what I wanted to do," Klaas said. "I wanted to talk with them parent to parent. I told Margaret Gregory there would be no cameras, just me."

Later Wednesday morning, Susan and David made their first public appearance in several days. Reporters and editors gathered around television sets in the newsroom as the couple tearfully pleaded for the safe return of their children. Neither of them took questions from reporters. Wells made it clear there would be no questions before David and Susan approached the microphones.

For me, this was a turning point. I thought Susan Smith gave a pitiful performance. While most people whose children had been missing for eight days would have been struggling to speak, I felt Susan Smith was struggling to cry.

"Whoever has my children . . . please, please bring them to us," Susan said. "Michael and Alex, your momma and daddy will be right here when you get home."

David asked the public to keep looking for his little boys.

"Keep your eyes open," he said. "And continue to pray for me and my wife. But most of all, pray for Michael and Alex."

Susan closed her statement this way:

"The night this happened, Michael did something he never did before," Susan said. "He said, 'I love you so much, Momma.' He told me he loved me before, but not without me telling him first. And I am clinging to that."

Within hours after David and Susan Smith pleaded for the return of their children on national television, law enforcement officers searched Susan's home on Toney Road. They removed several bags of evidence from a crawl space and inside the house.

Later in the day Brad Rogers asked me to join him outside for a breath of fresh air. He was going to smoke a cigarette and I would be the one getting the fresh air.

"What can we do to get this story moving?" Brad said as we sat down at a picnic table outside the *Herald-Journal* building. "How long can this go on without a break?"

I didn't have answers for either question.

When we returned to the newsroom, I placed a call to John Rabon, vice-president of the National Center for Missing and

Exploited Children in Arlington, Virginia. I'd seen Rabon on NBC's "Dateline" the previous night. I thought he might be able to help me with a new approach because his organization deals with these cases daily. Rabon seemed as confused as we were about Susan's story.

"Why would a black man steal her children?" he asked me. "This case is like Jell-O. The more you squeeze it, the less you have in your hand."

Rabon went on to say the chances that Alex and Michael had been harmed increased by the minute. "You've got to start looking at family members and friends," Rabon said. "They'll have to receive more investigation than before. About 98 percent of all abductions of children are committed by family members. It's rare for a child to be abducted by a stranger."

When I'd finished the interview, I wrote a story for the next day's paper about how Klaas had been turned away by Gregory, and I included the information from Rabon.

DAY IX

November 3, 1994

As the search for Alex and Michael Smith continued without results, frustrations were really beginning to build with the media. For days the news briefings had offered little new information. Reports had surfaced earlier in the week that some members of the media were getting ready to pull out of Union. It was getting more difficult for reporters to justify the tremendous expense of covering the event to their news directors and editors.

On Thursday morning, Susan and David Smith came out of hiding again. They were interviewed on all the early-morning network television shows live from the living room of the Russell's home in Mt. Vernon Estates. They pleaded again for the safe return of their children.

Sheriff Wells continued to meet with reporters twice each day – once about 9 a.m. and again late in the afternoon. He always looked as though his suit had been pressed and he'd just put on a fresh shirt and necktie before he started the news conferences. His shoes shined like freshly polished silver. He was articulate and carefully chose what information he gave the media. Many times, you could feel the tension as reporters pushed him for information. On the surface, he showed little emotion. But I often wondered how he must really feel as he walked away from the bank of microphones. Before this week he'd probably not been on television more than a few times. He was a fine ambassador for Union County.

"It's time to get on top of this story," Brad told reporter Reggie Fields and me at a meeting on Thursday morning. "Let's start at the beginning. Go back to people you've already talked with. Maybe they'll tell you more this time. But we've got to make this thing move."

Reggie and I went through our lists of sources and contacts in Union. We decided we would check in at the courthouse, but after that, we were going to keep moving. Each of us made a list of people we would see and places we would go. We would keep in touch by telephone but decided we would not give out any information over our two-way radios, just in case we were being monitored by competitors. Several times during the day one of us would page the other one and then meet somewhere to discuss what new information we had learned.

By this time in the investigation at least one *Herald-Journal* photographer was in Union 24 hours a day. Mike Bonner and Gerry Pate shared that duty.

On Thursday morning, photographer Thomas McCarver was assigned to work with Reggie and me for the day. The two of them drove to Union together, and I drove alone.

Reporters were already gathering for the morning news conference when I arrived at the courthouse. I'd witnessed this morning event for days, but for me, the atmosphere seemed different today. Some of the reporters seemed to be losing interest.

As soon as Wells finished, I headed to Putnam, a small farm community west of Union on Highway 215.

David Smith grew up in a small white house there. During the early part of the Smiths' marriage, he and Susan lived in the community with David's great-grandmother. I'd been there during the first week of the search for the boys to speak with Bobby Smith, who operates a one-man print shop just off Highway 215.

"I've known David since he was a little boy," said Smith, who is not related to either David or Susan. "He's a fine young man."

Smith talked about David's devotion to his great-grandmother and talked about problems the Smith family had faced early on. Since he had lived in Union County his entire life, I was hoping Bobby Smith might have heard some bit of information I could use. Major news stories are often broken because of some tip or rumor a reporter hears. But I heard none in Putnam.

As I was about to leave Smith's print shop, my pager beeped.

"We want you and Reggie to meet us at the Burger King in Union at 11:30 a.m.," Diane said when I called the newsroom. "Brad and I have talked about some other areas we want the two of you to explore."

Thomas, Reggie and I took advantage of the downtime at Burger King. While Diane and Brad talked about other things they would like us to check, we ate Whopper burgers. We knew it could be many hours before we would have the opportunity to eat again.

While our editors were making good points about people we needed to speak with or revisit, it was becoming more difficult to do so. For more than a week reporters had besieged Union like a swarm of locusts. People who earlier were willing to talk were now saying, "No comment." It was tough work.

My last stop was at the search command center about two blocks from the courthouse. Officials had moved the center from the courthouse to the Union County Parks and Recreation Building on Wednesday because they needed more room.

Yellow police tape prevented anyone from entering from the front side of the parking lot outside areas set aside for SLED, FBI and sheriff's investigators. But no tape had been put up at the rear of the building and the gate leading into the parking lot was open. So I walked in, just as FBI agent Charlie Shepard walked toward his car. It was one of the few cars in the parking lot. And that fact bothered me.

"Where is everybody, Charlie?" I asked him. "It's a little lonely around here."

Shepard is a friendly man with a quick smile. He doesn't fit the image I have of how I think an FBI agent should look.

"Gary, you know I can't tell you that," said Shepard, smiling.

"Well, where are you going?"

"To get some lunch."

Two other officers walked out the door. A CBS News crew on the other side of the yellow tape got the attention of one of them, and the other one told me I was in a restricted area.

I walked back outside the gate. A news crew from a Georgia television station was there, and so was Susan Scarborough, a WSPA-TV reporter. Several other newspaper reporters had also arrived.

"What did he tell you, Gary?" asked Susan, with a grin. "Is something about to happen?"

She said it half jokingly, but I knew she was getting the same pressure I was from her bosses. And she knew I would not share anything of importance the police might have told me. If I had been in her place I would have asked the same question.

"He said he was going to lunch, Susan," I said, with a chuckle.

We stood there watching the activity at the command center for a few moments. Then I decided to take another drive around town to see if I could observe any change in routine. "See you," I said as I turned to walk to my car.

"He knows something," she said to her cameraman. "Let's go."

As I turned my car around in the middle of the street and drove away, the WSPA-TV van followed me. All I need is a television van following me everywhere I go, I thought. When I reached the courthouse, I drove into the parking lot past the WYFF-TV mobile studio, past the NBC News mobile home studio, and out the back entrance. No van in sight.

I knew why Susan was so curious. When you follow news events long enough you develop a sense of knowing when a change has taken place. I was beginning to get that feeling.

For awhile, I drove along side streets and then returned to Main. The traffic was bumper to bumper. It seemed I would never reach the north end of town.

Finally, I approached the sign on North Main Street that points to Veterans Park and Union High School and made a left turn. I wanted to see if there was any activity at David Smith's apartment. For a week I had checked it several times daily. Numerous knocks on the door had gone unanswered. It was the same today.

After sitting in the parking lot for awhile, I drove back toward downtown. On the way, I decided to drive by Susan Smith's house on Toney Road. It appeared undisturbed. Alex and Michael's toys were still scattered all around in the carport. It had the same bleak appearance every time I saw it. I wondered when was the last time the boys played with the toys.

It was nearing 3 p.m. and I decided to check in at the press center outside the sheriff's office. As I drove on Highway 176 toward downtown, two South Carolina Highway Patrol cars passed me.

Suddenly, it struck me. I had seen an unusual number of state troopers on this last trip around the area. I wondered why so many of them were in Union.

The press area was packed when I reached downtown. I had trouble finding a place to park. Network television correspondents were already sending satellite reports to their affiliates for the noon news shows on the west coast.

In just over an hour, *Herald-Journal* editors and staff members would begin the daily 4 p.m. budget meeting to discuss the following day's newspaper. This is the time when decisions are made on how stories will be played or positioned for the following day.

"Well, we came up dry," Reggie told me. "How about you?"

"I'm afraid I didn't do any better," I replied, looking at the activity around us. "But this sure is a busy place. I guess we'll write 'The Search Continues.' "

Photographer Mike Bonner had joined us. He had been driving around town as well.

"They are dragging the lake again," Bonner said. "They have barricades up this time and the highway patrol has blocked the entrance."

For the next 30 minutes or so, we talked with other reporters and waited. A prayer meeting of Union ministers was scheduled for 5:30 p.m. outside the sheriff's office. So far, that was the highlight of what we had to report for Friday's newspaper. Just before 4 p.m I walked to Bonner's van to call the newsroom.

"Nothing's changed," I told Brad Rogers. "No one's talking. Reggie and I stayed out all day, but we got nowhere."

"Oh, well," he said with a sigh. He knew Reggie and I had worked hard to find something new, but Brad is a master at making reporters feel guilty for not having a sensational story everyday. "We'll see you up here after the news conference."

"Of course Brad is real happy with us," I said to Reggie, as I returned to the area where he was standing with Thomas McCarver, Bonner and WYFF-TV reporter Bill Wilson. Reggie smiled, knowing the gist of my conversation with our city editor.

Wilson walked away to prepare for his 5 p.m. newscast, and I was about to go inside to a drinking fountain in the hallway by the sheriff's office.

As I turned, the small black pager on the waistband of my pants and those of every *Herald-Journal* staff member near me activated. The digital printout on all of them read 7229, Brad Rogers' phone number at the city desk. I turned and ran toward Bonner's van. The others followed me.

"Susan has confessed," Brad almost yelled into the phone. "She killed the boys. They found the car in the lake."

I had him pause long enough for me to tell the others what I had learned.

"Hurry, so I can go back to the lake," said Bonner, urging me to end the telephone conversation.

"Tell Reggie to get on to the Russells' house and you stay at the courthouse," Brad continued. "I'm sending Suellen. I'll tell her to look for you at the courthouse."

I hung up the telephone and walked alone back to the area where we had been standing on the sidewalk. Main Street was getting jammed with cars. The word was spreading fast.

Bonner jumped in his van and headed back to the lake. The entrance was blocked by 10 to 15 highway patrol officers, and police cars lined both sides of the road. Yellow crime-scene tape stretched across the entrance and extended into the woods on both sides of the road leading to the boat ramp. A crowd gathered and listened to their car radios for information.

The scene at the courthouse was just as frantic. As I watched, a feeling of nausea moved out of my stomach and made its way throughout my body.

"She did it, she really did it," I said quietly to myself.

But I did not have time to grieve. That would come later. For now, I had to go to work.

It was much later before I knew how Brad learned Susan Smith had confessed to killing her children. It was ironic the newsroom knew about her confession before those of us on the scene in Union.

It happened this way. *Herald-Journal* reporter Shelly Haskins was in Spartanburg City Hall on an unrelated story. Assistant Public Information Director Stewart Burgess asked him, "Did you hear about the kids? They found them and they are dead. The mother did it."

Burgess told Shelly the report had just been broadcast on a "secured" police radio frequency. Newsrooms monitor other police and emergency channels, but we are unable to monitor the "secured" channels.

The city hall in Spartanburg is located on Broad Street, less than a city block from the *Herald-Journal* employee entrance. Shelly ran back to the newsroom and straight into the budget meeting where editors were deciding what story would lead Friday's front page. They no longer had to make that decision. Susan Smith made it for them.

The news about Susan Smith's confession spread quickly through the media area. Apparently, the *Associated Press* had moved an unconfirmed bulletin. Traffic on Main Street had become impossible. Television technicians were running about to get microphones and cameras in place for the news conference when Wells would make everything official.

While all this was going on, the television reporters were getting ready to go live with a news bulletin. Normal programming was interrupted throughout the nation. CNN was live on "Headline News" world-wide. Every satellite truck had a reporter standing along side it, talking live from Union, South Carolina.

I crossed over Main Street and claimed a spot close to where I knew Wells would stand during the news conference. From there I waited and watched as Union residents gathered outside the fence that separated the news area from the sidewalk. During the week, a few people had gathered from time to time to speak with reporters, but now the sidewalk was jammed. People were beginning to crowd into the area reserved for the media.

Other newspaper reporters began moving in to claim a spot as well. A few of the television reporters did live shots for their 6 p.m. news shows from the news conference site. Others filled the news conference area shortly after that.

By 6 p.m. you could barely move. People had pushed in from all sides. There were a few tense moments when reporters tried to reclaim space they had used for days. Photographer Gerry Pate had joined the crowd and was shooting the scene as fast as his cameras would operate.

"Gary, back here," I heard someone behind me yell. Suellen Dean was just getting to the courthouse. "Traffic was bad. I'm parked a mile away. Where do you need me?"

I was afraid to move closer because I was afraid I would lose my place. So I yelled back to her.

"I've got this covered and Reggie is at the Russells," I told her. "See if you can help Bonner at the lake and then come back here. We'll all need to be here when it's over."

It had been two hours since I had spoken to anyone in the newsroom, but getting out of Union on a cellular telephone was impossible.

"Do you have your phone in your van?" I asked Suellen. "Try to tell the city desk what we are doing."

Pat Wright, a woman I know from Spartanburg, was standing several feet behind me. She was working security for the television show "American Journal."

"Here, Gary, try mine," said Pat as she passed a telephone to me. It was no use. I could not complete the call. It was telephone gridlock. I could only assume Brad and the other editors in Spartanburg knew we had it under control.

An evening chill settled in with the darkness. You could see your breath. I was glad I had gone to my car for a jacket earlier. The atmosphere was charged with emotion. You could feel it. Veteran reporters looked stunned.

As we waited, I looked as far as I could see up and down Main Street. Satellite dishes and microwave arms stretched toward the heavens with a ghostly reach. Television lights cast ominous glows in patterns along the street and all around us.

"Have you ever covered a local event that became this kind of national story?" I asked ABC News Corespondent Mike Von Fremd, who was standing next to me.

"Yes I have," he answered. "When a little girl named Jessica fell in a well in Texas, it was this big. I was there the night they got her out."

Von Fremd was one of the people who had been able to get a cellular telephone call out of Union that night. Once he got through to ABC News Control Center in New York, he kept the line open.

"They are coming directly to you from Peter," a technician yelled to Von Fremd, meaning as soon as the ABC Evening News with Peter Jennings was on the air, Jennings would introduce Von Fremd in Union.

But at 6:30 p.m. Wells had not shown up. Von Fremd asked them over the telephone to delay. Jennings read other news while the crowd waited for the sheriff.

Von Fremd and I never spoke again that night. He seemed absorbed in his own thoughts and I needed a little time to prepare for what we were about to hear as well.

As I stood there quietly, I looked at the wide arc of 40 television cameras pointed toward the bank of microphones. I had only one thought at the moment.

The whole world is watching us in Union tonight.

Suddenly a reporter standing by one of the television cameras said, "Heads up, here they come."

As Sheriff Howard Wells and SLED Chief Robert Stewart walked toward the microphones, you could hear the television reporters introducing the scene viewers were watching. Howard Wells seemed to be exhausted, but he spoke with the same authority he became known for throughout the search. He spoke methodically and controlled the few moments he was in front of the army of reporters.

And then he read:

> "Susan Smith has been arrested and will be charged with two counts of murder in connection with the deaths of her children, Michael, 3, and Alexander, 14 months.

A loud gasp rose from the crowd. Wells continued:

> "The vehicle, a 1990 Mazda, driven by Smith was located late Thursday afternoon in Lake John D. Long near Union. Two bodies were found in the vehicle's back seat. Identities are pending an autopsy.
>
> "Charges against Smith will be signed by Union County Sheriff Howard Wells.
>
> "Sixteenth Circuit Solicitor Thomas Pope said Thursday a bond hearing will be held Friday at 10 a.m. at the Moss Justice Center in York before Circuit Judge Henry Floyd.
>
> "Smith is incarcerated at an undisclosed location."

When Wells finished reading the statement, he and Stewart turned and walked back inside the courthouse to the sheriff's office. They took no questions from reporters.

For a moment, there was stunned silence from the shocked and disbelieving crowd. Susan Smith's betrayal was complete. She had killed her own children.

The brief moment of dark silence was broken by the voice of Gilliam Edwards, a large black man I'd seen around the courthouse almost every day. Like the other times when I'd seen him, he wore a white neck brace. His voice reverberated off the walls around us.

"Speak up, black people. Don't be afraid!" Edwards shouted in a deep and loud voice. "They have accused us of murdering these children. They've done everything they could to us."

Police officers quickly surrounded the man and ushered him across the street and into a building, away from the crowd. All the time when the police officers were pushing him across the crowded street, he continued to yell.

Then it seemed as though everyone started speaking at once. It was difficult to hear people when they answered questions I had asked them.

No one left. They wandered about for more than an hour. The terrible announcement they came to hear was over. Now, they tried to make the horror and the loneliness of this moment go away by reaching out to one another.

The night was filled with weeping in Union, South Carolina.

"I'm heading back to the newsroom," I said to Reggie. "I'll get started on the news story and you can fill in whatever you have."

Reggie and I would write Friday's lead story under a double byline. That way our readers would get the most facts possible in our report. A day that started out with little news had now produced one of the most read newspapers of the entire nine-day search.

Reggie, a black man about the age of the composite Susan Smith gave police, wrote a sidebar story on the reaction of Union's black residents. Suellen wrote another sidebar on the feelings of people throughout the community.

I walked back to my car, threw my reporter's notebook in the right front seat and headed for the *Herald-Journal* newsroom.

As I drove out of town on Highway 176 toward Spartanburg, I crossed Toney Road. I was about two blocks from where Susan Smith had lived in a small brick-veneer home with Alex and Michael. Until two months earlier the boys' father, David Smith, had lived there too. I reached down and turned off the car radio. It was a good night to drive back to Spartanburg in silence.

Just knowing I stood 100 feet from where Susan Smith's car rested on the floor of the lake, with the boys still strapped upside down in their car seats would cause sleepless nights for weeks. I dreaded the dreams and nightmares I knew would come.

It was almost 9 p.m. when I reached the newsroom. Managing editor Scott Kearns was standing near my desk dressed in jeans and sneakers. He had already gone home for dinner and returned. I knew why he had come back. This was one of those nights he wanted to "put the paper to bed," meaning he would not leave until he saw the Friday's proofs.

"Are you okay?" Scott asked me as I walked toward him.

"Sure, I'm okay. It's just hard to believe she did it."

"You know, Gary, I told you she did this all along."

"Yeah, I know you did, and I knew it, too," I said. "But it doesn't make it any easier."

Scott is the father of two teenaged children. He has not forgotten how a reporter can feel covering a tough assignment such as this one. And he knows what the reader wants.

"Use some front page words and write it from here," Scott said as he pointed to his heart. "Let them feel it."

My fellow reporters Reggie Fields and Suellen Dean walked in soon after I did. Suellen, the mother of two little girls, stopped at my work station.

"You know, Gary, I had to pull off the road and cry on the way back," she said. "I don't even know how long I sat there. But I guess you understand, don't you?"

I understood.

BLUE AND WHITE BOWS

November 4, 1994

Friday morning's headline recalled the dreadful moment I'd experienced in Union the previous night.

"Mother confesses, two boys are dead."

The bold words ran across the top of the page with a photograph of Alex and Michael to the left of it. A photograph of Susan Smith, the boys' 23-year-old mother, was to the right of the headline. The photograph of Smith's burgundy four-door Mazda was pictured in the middle of the page. A large chunk of mud was stuck to the left rear wheel.

Bonner had taken the photograph as the car was hauled away on the rear of a tow truck. Below his photograph of the car a black woman and a white man were shown in a photograph taken at the moment Howard Wells read his statement. Both faces expressed unbelievable shock. A tear rolled down the woman's face and dripped from her cheek.

Friday was a homecoming of sorts for Susan Smith. Her scheduled hearing in York, where she was kept overnight, was changed to the Union County Courthouse. Suellen Dean, Steve Shultz and I were assigned to cover Smith's return to Union for arraignment. Suellen's assignment was to write a profile of the woman who had drowned her children. She spent the entire day trying to gather information from friends, former teachers and anyone else who would talk about their memories of Susan Smith. Steve went to restaurants and everywhere people gathered to write what they were feeling on this sad Friday.

Molly McDonough, in her first weeks as a court reporter with the *Herald-Journal*, was assigned to cover proceedings inside the courthouse.

I couldn't believe it was already 6 a.m. when the clock sounded that Friday morning. For several days, I had gotten by on four to five hours of sleep each night, but I was beginning to feel it.

"You'll need to drive Heather this morning," Carmela said. "I'll plan to pick her up because I know you'll not be back in time."

Heather, our 19-year-old daughter, was a sophomore at the University of South Carolina-Spartanburg. She usually drove her car to school, but Carmela needed to run an errand at noon-time so she borrowed Heather's car for the day.

I was glad I was taking my daughter to class. It gave me an opportunity to spend some time with her and talk. After learning the terrible news the night before I needed to be near her. I could not tell her enough how much I loved her that Friday morning.

Thankfully, Carmela and I are close to both our children. We enjoy a relationship that other parents have told us they envy.

"I guess I'll see you late tonight," I told Heather as she got out of the car. And once again I said, "Heather, I love you."

She threw her backpack over her shoulder, told me good-bye, and walked across the parking lot to the grassy lawn in the middle of the campus. As I watched her, I sat in my car and wept.

My assignment was to cover Susan's arrival for her arraignment and her departure for the Women's Correctional Center in Columbia. She had been held overnight at the York County Detention Center. A crowd was already on hand when I reached the courthouse about 8:45 a.m.

"Security is tight today," said Bonner, pointing toward two sharpshooters with rifles on the courthouse roof. "Look at that."

But the marksmen weren't the only signs of increased security. Yellow tape and several Union County sheriff's officers prevented us from going inside the parking lot that had served as a media compound for the last 10 days.

Less than an hour later, police were forced to close the block of Main Street in front of the courthouse. People filled the sidewalks and spilled over into the street, at times blocking traffic.

While I waited for Susan to arrive at the courthouse, I walked through the crowd and talked with people. All of them expressed sorrow and grief, but many of them expressed outrage for Susan Smith.

But none of them spoke like 43-year-old Edna Meadow, a black woman from Union. Her grasp of what had taken place was the best of anyone I spoke to.

"It's not a race thing here," she said, referring to the way Smith had said a black man kidnapped her children. "This is all about how them pitiful babies left this world."

Mrs. Meadow, the mother of six children, held her 3-year-old granddaughter, Whitney, as she spoke.

"My heart goes out for them babies," said the woman as her eyes filled with tears. "When you kill a child, you kill one of God's little angels."

By now, the crowd had grown to several hundred, and the air was charged with tension. In the distance, I heard sirens make their yelping sound briefly and then cease. When I turned to look south on Main Street, I saw a line of fast-moving police cars coming toward the courthouse.

Susan Smith was back in Union.

Officers tried to keep the crowd back as the police cars turned slowly into the parking lot by the sheriff's office. But it was no use. People moved in so tight the cars could barely get through. Susan Smith was in the second car. She buried her face in a coat as the cars turned.

"I'd hide my face, too," yelled a middle-aged woman. "You bitch." And then a chant that started on the courthouse lawn quickly spread to the crowd onto the street.

"Murderer, murderer, murderer."

A few days earlier, the crowd that came to this same place to hear Susan Smith plead for the safe return of her children had cried for her.

Inside the courthouse, about 150 reporters and onlookers watched as Susan Smith was arraigned for the murders of her two little boys. Everyone who entered the hearing had to pass through a metal detector. SLED and sheriff's officers lined all sides of the courtroom. The old dark furnishings in the room gave the place a feeling of historic importance in the 82-year-old building. Clearly, Susan Smith was writing her own page of Union County history. She was only in the courthouse for about two hours. Family members visited with her and she was then taken to the Women's Correctional Center in Columbia.

When she was gone, I made another visit to the Clerk of Courts Office inside the courthouse. This time, I picked up a copy of Susan Smith's arrest warrant. The last line under the description of her offense read: "Probable cause being based on a confession by the defendant." Howard Wells had taken Susan to Union's First Baptist Church where he confronted her with the inconsistencies in her story. She told him where they would find Alex and Michael. Wells returned to the lake to see for himself. Then he and Robert Stewart boarded a SLED helicopter and flew to the Russell home to officially tell the families. The pilot landed the helicopter in the Russell's back yard. The 42-year-old sheriff is a long-time friend with Bev Russell.

On Friday, it was several hours before people began to drift away from the courthouse. Up in the business section of Main Street a transformation was taking place. Yellow ribbons were being replaced by blue and white bows.

"The blue is for the little boys, and the white is for their innocence," 21-year-old Carla Williams told me as she tied a bow to her store front. "Their mother made a fool out of everybody."

As the yellow ribbons were being changed to blue and white bows, an old model Ford pickup truck drove along Main Street. Its owner had attached this hand-lettered sign to the tailgate:

"Michael and Alex are safe in the arms of Jesus. We love you."

I was emotionally drained when I sat down to write the lead story for Saturday morning's *Herald-Journal*. Scott saw me come in and walked over to my desk. Again, he gave sound advice.

"Put me in the car with her," Scott said. "Use front page words."

As I turned on my computer terminal, I had this thought.

"Today was Union's first day of healing."

On Friday night the Union High School Yellow Jackets football team defeated the Boiling Springs Bulldogs from Spartanburg County 13-10. There was talk of canceling the game, but instead, the crowd stood and observed a moment of silence for Alex and Michael Smith. It was a good idea to play the game. It gave the people of Union County two hours of relief from the hurt and grief they felt so deeply.

RESPECTS

November 5, 1995

Light showers and cool temperatures arrived with the dawn on Saturday morning in Upstate South Carolina. By midday, skies were clearing.

Reggie Fields and Janet Spencer were assigned to cover the events in Union. I had a day of rest to prepare for Sunday's funeral coverage.

Reggie went to John D. Long Lake on Saturday. So did hundreds of other people. Some of them had driven great distances to pay their respects to two little boys they never knew.

Flower sprays from as far away as Minneapolis were scattered about the boat ramp area. The words written on a card attached to a spray of blue and white flowers from New Orleans read: "We love you in New Orleans."

Reggie's report of his visit to the lake was moving. In the afternoon, he attended the taping of the "Oprah Winfrey Show" at the Buffalo United Methodist Church. Her show was only one of several television talk shows that aired from Union during the two weeks of the search and immediately after Susan Smith's confession.

On Saturday morning Holcombe Funeral Home workers placed the single casket that held the bodies of Michael and Alex Smith in a viewing room. People began coming by to see the closed casket as early as 10 a.m.

A visitation scheduled for Saturday evening at the funeral home was attended by hundreds. The event was supposed to end at 9 p.m., but more than 150 people were still in line. David Smith and other family members agreed to stay until all of them had the opportunity to walk through the receiving line.

A woman from Clinton, South Carolina, who had driven 70 miles to attend the visitation, told Janet Spencer, "We don't know them. We just want to pay our respects to their sons."

MOURNING

November 6, 1994

Rain that began falling in the dark hours continued as I showered and dressed on Sunday morning. I was hoping the weather reports were correct. Clearing was expected by midday.

"This is going to be harder for everybody if the rain continues," I said to Carmela as I ate a stack of pancakes for breakfast. "Maybe the funeral today will help a lot of people gain some closure with this."

For some, it probably did help bring the long and tragic event to a close. I've continued to cover David Smith and have gotten to know him. Months later, I still make an occasional trip to John D. Long Lake to see the place his children died.

"Think about me. It's going to be a tough day," I said to Carmela and Heather. Then I was out the back door.

On the way out of town, I stopped briefly at the *Herald-Journal* newsroom to pickup a fresh reporter's notebook. It was early and the employee parking lot was empty. Passing cars made a splashing sound on the wet streets. Upstairs, the newsroom was quiet, except for the police and fire scanners that seem never to stop, even on Sunday morning.

There was little traffic on Highway 176 as I drove to Union. The rain had stopped and the sky looked as though it might clear. I knew I would be early, but I had planned to attend the 11 a.m. services at the Buffalo United Methodist Church. I wanted to give myself some time to drive around Union before I went to the church. I knew the service would be crowded and I wanted to make sure I got inside for the service – and for Alex and Michael's funeral at 2 p.m. I think almost everybody in Union went to church that Sunday. Churches all over town were full. Everybody in Union was praying for Alex and Michael that day.

At St. Paul Baptist Church, a predominately black congregation, the Rev. A. L. Brackett told worshipers, "My message today is that we are dealing with the healing process. The healing must continue."

At Grace United Methodist Church the Rev. Bob Waddell also consoled his congregation. During the children's sermon, the pastor's voice broke as he told the children gathered around him that Alex and Michael were in heaven.

> "There, these children will escape war and find everlasting peace," Waddell said. "No sin shall darken their lives, and no cry of pain shall ever touch their lips."

After a brief trip through downtown Union, I left for the five-minute drive to Buffalo United Methodist Church. A short distance after I passed the United Merchants Mill, I turned onto Church Street leading off Highway 215 to the sanctuary. The street was lined with neat mill village houses. Majestic oak trees reached out to form a canopy from both sides of the street. For today, someone had stretched blue ribbons around each tree and tied them off with blue bows.

I went into the church and sat down on the last pew. Don

Sider, a writer with *People* magazine followed me. Jenny Munro with the *Greenville News* and Chris Burritt with the *Atlanta Constitution* sat in front of us.

When the service was over, very few people left the church. The ones who planned to attend the funeral knew if they left they might not get a seat. A long line of people who wanted to get inside for the funeral had waited outside the church since early morning.

I was glad I had two hours to wait. It gave me time to reflect on what I'd experienced as both a reporter and human being in the last 10 days.

Sider and I talked quietly for awhile and then I asked him to hold my seat. I knew I would not get a chance to eat until after I got back to Spartanburg, so I slipped quietly to the men's room and took out a package of Pop Tarts I'd put in the breast pocket of my suit coat. I ate one and saved the other one for later. I eventually gave it to a reporter who had not eaten all day.

When I returned to my seat I was glad I'd asked Sider to hold it for me. Even more people had arrived and a large section of pews was being reserved for the families.

Loudspeakers were set up in the church dining hall and outside the church building. Several thousand people stood together on the church lawn and on the streets in the warm November afternoon.

Just before 1 p.m. the casket containing the bodies of Alex and Michael Smith was rolled to the front of the church. A large spray of yellow roses and an 8 x 10 photograph of the two boys was placed on top of it.

Then ushers allowed people who could not get a seat to come inside the church for a last visit with the little boys. For more than an hour they came. Some would pause long enough to say a silent prayer and touch the casket. All of them wept as they left the church.

"I have children at home the age of these little boys," said a woman near me as people continued to file by the casket. "Maybe that's why it hurts so much."

She was expressing familiar thoughts. Even though my children are much older, there were many times during this week of horrors I reflected on how much I truly care for them.

An elderly woman seated behind us in one of the chairs that had been placed in the auditorium told me she had driven all night to be here for the funeral.

"I lost twins when they were 16 years old," Ferroll Craig of Newport News, Virginia, told me. "It hurts so much to see these young lives snuffed out so needlessly. I was compelled to be here. God wants me here."

Outside, the funeral procession was arriving. Bonner had stationed himself directly across from the doors of the church. His view through the camera lens was sometimes almost blurred by tears. For him, the event moved in milliseconds and was over. All he could do was point his camera and shoot.

Just before the 2 p.m. service began, two small boys walked to the front of the church and stared briefly at the photograph of Michael and Alex that rested on their casket. Then as they turned to leave, the older boy reached down and took his companion's hand. They walked out of the church in silence.

The two little boys were the last mourners to visit the casket before the family arrived and were seated in the pews. To me it seemed fitting the last two people to stand by the casket in the church that Sunday afternoon were two small children.

Within moments after the two little boys walked out of the sanctuary, family members arrived and were ushered to their seats. David Smith led the long line of people. His uncle, Doug Smith, and his step-mother, Susan Smith, supported him by his arms and helped him walk to the front of the church.

"I don't believe I've ever seen anyone grieving like that," I said to the woman seated near me. "How will he get through this?"

Throughout the service, expressions of grief and sorrow covered the faces of everyone inside the church. There was one time when the emotions were overwhelming.

When the music box sounds of "Jesus Loves Me" and "Away in a Manger" were played, it was impossible to hold back the tears.

"Oh, the boys won't be here for Christmas," said a woman standing at the rear of the church.

As she spoke, the Rev. Bob Cato walked to the podium.

"Last Tuesday night, I met with David and his family," said Cato, his voice strained with emotion. "They said, 'We want our boys home.' "

Then Cato paused as he struggled to speak.

"The boys are home."

When the service was over, David Smith followed his children's casket as it was rolled slowly from the church and loaded into a steel-grey hearse for the seven-mile ride to the Bogansville United Methodist Church Cemetery in West Springs, South Carolina. Just before he reached the funeral service family car, David Smith turned for a final look at his sons' rose-draped casket.

When I went inside the Buffalo United Methodist Church five hours earlier, only a handful of television cameras were set up outside. When I walked out moments before the service ended, I faced at least 40 of them. They represented not only local stations, but every national television network as well.

Knowing the streets around the church would be congested, I had parked my car near the corner of Highway 215 and Church Street on Sunday morning. It was a short walk and I wanted to be able to leave quickly so I could be at the cemetery when the funeral procession arrived.

"Thomas is at the cemetery and Matthew is somewhere on the road between here and there," said photographer Gerry Pate, referring to *Herald-Journal* photographers Thomas McCarver and Matthew Fortner. "I'll see you in Spartanburg tonight."

Five *Herald-Journal* photographers were assigned to work Michael and Alex Smith's funeral, including free-lance photographer David Rentas. It was Rentas who captured the photo of David Smith as he left Buffalo United Methodist Church following the funeral. His dramatic photograph showing the young father in the deepest grief imaginable led Monday's paper.

After I spoke briefly with Gerry Pate, I walked back to my car and headed west on Highway 215 toward Bogansville. I was not expecting what I saw along the way.

Almost every mailbox along the rural stretch of highway had a blue bow attached to it. People stood in their yards, sat on porches and waited by the side of the road to watch as Michael and Alex passed. Some of the people held signs that said,

"We love you and will never forget you, Alex and Michael."

Near the small farm village of Putnam, where David and Susan Smith lived when they were first married, a man and a boy stood silently by the road. The boy held a large bouquet of helium-filled blue and white balloons.

The funeral procession was one of the longest anyone could remember in Union County. Fourteen police cars from the Union County Sheriff's Office, the State Law Enforcement Division, Union City Police and the South Carolina Department of Natural

Resources led the long line of mourners on their seven-mile journey. The cars were filled with police officers and divers who had participated in the search for Michael and Alex.

Several thousand people waited at the cemetery for the funeral procession to arrive. Again, the television cameras were there. The funeral was carried live on television stations throughout South Carolina.

The service at the cemetery was brief. As the final prayer ended, two balloons drifted slowly toward the heavens. David Smith rose from his chair and then knelt to kiss his little boys' casket.

"I don't want to leave, I don't want to leave," he moaned as two family members helped him walk toward the waiting car.

Once inside, David clutched a photograph of 3-year-old Michael and 14-month-old Alex tightly to his chest, then fell forward in uncontrollable grief.

In a county of 33,000 people, police estimate 5,000 to 6,000 participated in some part of the funeral for Alex and Michael.

"We were hoping it would not end this way," Lt. Jeff Lawson of the Union County Sheriff's Office told me, with tears streaming down his face. "It was a long search."

The media was not allowed under the funeral tents during the service. I stood a few feet away with my friend and fellow-reporter Jenny Munro of the *Greenville News*. Jenny covers Spartanburg for her newspaper, and usually we are competitors. But on this day we stood with our arms around one another for support, as we watched the final chapter in a tragic story come to a close.

This scene in a country church cemetery was the end of a day of mourning for the community, the state and the nation. South

Carolina Governor Carroll Campbell had declared Sunday as a day of mourning.

More than 700 sprays of flowers were sent to the funeral from people as far away as Puerto Rico and New Zealand. One had come from Washington, D.C. The card on it read: "The President and Mrs. Clinton."

"Alex and Michael died on my birthday," Carrie Waite, a 35-year-old woman from Chattanooga, Tennessee, told me. "I don't know why, but I had to come here. I'll always have a reminder of them every year."

Elizabeth Kingsmore, an 80-year-old woman who has lived her entire life in Union County expressed her feelings this way: "All these people that came here, they'll go away. But for we that live here, this is hard. It's going to stay with us. We'll try to forget, but it will be hard."

For a long time after the boys' family had gone, people walked around the grave site and looked at the hundreds of flower arrangements. If they spoke, it was in hushed tones.

Like these people, I found it difficult to leave the cemetery that Sunday afternoon. For two weeks the search for Michael and Alex Smith had occupied most of my waking hours. Even though I never knew them, I found it difficult to let them go.

However, I had a deadline facing me in the newsroom. When I left Bogansville, I continued west on Highway 215 back to Spartanburg. I had not spoken with anyone in the newsroom since early Sunday morning.

"I'm on the way back," I told Diane as I drove through the Glenn Springs community. "I have a lot of stuff, so I'm going to need some space."

"Don't worry about that," she replied. "Come on in and let's get rolling."

During the rest of the drive, I thought about how I would write the story. I practiced several story "leads," but I decided to just tell it from my heart as I had seen it unfold.

Several people were gathered around a television watching the news when I walked to my desk. Diane walked by and asked, "Are you all right?"

I told her, "Yes, I think I'm fine. It was just a difficult day."

Then I sat down to write the lead story for Monday morning's *Herald-Journal*. I didn't want anything to delay me. I wanted to remember every detail I'd seen that day.

As I logged on to the computer, newsroom clerk and close friend Sylvia Deakin stopped me. Sylvia grew up in Maine. After more than 20 years in the South, she has lost little of her New England accent. The nine days had been difficult for her as well. She has three grandchildren, one that is close in age to Michael. Several times during the week she expressed her sad feelings to me when I returned from Union. Sylvia is one the kindest people I know and liked by everyone in the newsroom. She is like a grandmother for many of us who work there. Her encouragement has often lifted my tired spirits. This day was no different.

"Gary, stand up," Sylvia said softly. As I did, she placed her arms around me. "You don't start writing this one until I have given you a hug."

After a long embrace with my friend, I turned and walked into the solitude of the men's room near my desk. Alone, I wept for two little boys from Union, South Carolina, who had become everybody's children.

About an hour after I started writing the story, the message light on my computer screen flashed. I cleared the screen and read the message:

"I cried for Alex and Michael today and I cried for Susan, too. Because in her sane moments, she will be driven insane by the deed she has done. KEARNS"

To this day, we've never discussed the message. I knew it was Scott's way of telling me the pain was shared.

I finished writing my story and pushed the computer key that sent it on to the city desk.

"Okay, Diane, you've got it," I said as I walked across the newsroom for a fresh cup of coffee. "I'll wait around to see if you have questions."

While I waited, I put my reporter's notebook into a thick file marked "Alex and Michael" and placed it in a drawer. Scott walked by and stopped at my desk.

"Thanks for doing a good job," Scott said. "I know it's been a tough two weeks."

A November chill wrapped tightly around me as I picked up Monday morning's newspaper on my front lawn. I returned to the dining room light and read the headline aloud:

"Union Says Goodbye to Alex and Michael –
The Boys Are Home."

Scott was right. It had been two weeks filled with disappointment, tears, sometimes a little hope, bone-deep fatigue, and in the end, enough grief and loneliness for a long time to come.

EPILOGUE

Six months have passed since Alex and Michael Smith died. I still think about the autumn days I spent in Union, South Carolina, covering their story. Police were deep into the nine-day search before I gave up hope they'd be found alive. I suppose the yellow ribbons on Main Street had something to do with that. The day people put them up I remember thinking how I'd write the story of Alex and Michael's welcome home parade. It never happened. Instead of cheers, there were tears on Main Street.

On Monday, the day following the boys' funeral, I was the first person to arrive at the newsroom. For a long time I just sat at my desk and drank coffee. Brad Rogers' voice broke the silence in the room just after 8 a.m.

"I've done pretty well with this until I read your funeral story," said Rogers, the father of two small children. "That one got me."

Other reporters and news staff arrived for work. Everyone talked about the funeral and how sad Sunday seemed. Alex and Michael's story had touched us all.

In mid-November, Bonner and I returned to Union. Jesse Jackson came into town to speak to churches and students at Union High School. The purpose of his visit was to soothe any lingering thoughts of anger about Susan telling police a black man took her children.

It was also the day Bonner and I returned to John D. Long Lake. We went our own ways when we got out of the van. I think both of us were trying to close the door on this story. For a long time I looked out across the peaceful water. When it was time to leave, I whispered, "Goodbye, Alex and Michael."

On the way back to Spartanburg, Bonner and I stopped for another look at the boys' grave in the Bogansville Cemetery. After a moment, we were ready to leave. It was time to lock the door we'd closed at the lake.

Within days after the funeral, the world's focus shifted to 24-year-old David Smith. Susan was locked away at the Women's Correctional Facility and Michael and Alex were buried in the cemetery at Bogansville United Methodist Church. Now, people wanted to know how the young father would go on with his life, but learning that was almost impossible.

David hired Michael Turner, a lawyer from Laurens, South Carolina, to represent him. Turner completely shut out the local media. He did broker interviews with ABC, CBS, and NBC, and after that David Smith went out of sight. All three interviews were conducted in Laurens and aired within days of each other, about two weeks after the funeral. When pressure from the local media to see David became intense, Turner called a news conference in his office.

"I'm here to answer questions you may want to ask of David," Turner said to me outside his office.

"That's great, Mike," I said, "but it probably comes as no surprise that you are not the one I want to speak with."

There were a few tense moments, but Turner answered questions for about an hour for several members of the local media. Most of the questions dealt with the Smiths' impending divorce, David's welfare and why he went to the national media and not the local newspapers and television. Turner said the national media got their message out more quickly. He told us the television interviews, which were all done in one day, were very difficult for David emotionally.

For the next three months I left numerous messages on David's answering machine at his apartment. Several times I knocked at his door and left business cards. On one Sunday afternoon in December, he answered the door and we spoke briefly. He said he was not in the mood to talk that day, but as always, David was friendly with me.

Throughout the time, I maintained frequent telephone contact with David's father and stepmother in California and with his uncle, Doug Smith in Michigan. My relationship with Doug began with a conversation we had in the sheriff's office parking lot, just a couple of days after the funeral. He was acting as spokesman for David's family. I gave him a business card and told him I'd appreciate an opportunity to talk with his nephew.

David returned to work at the Winn-Dixie Marketplace on the third shift in late November. Since the late shift had less shoppers, he would be bothered less by the curious. He took time off during the Christmas holidays and traveled to California to visit with his family. They took trips to Yellowstone and San Francisco. Susan Smith, David's stepmother, said they tried to keep David busy.

Christmas Day was the two-month anniversary of Alex and Michael's deaths. My family and I were back in Charleston for the holidays. Throughout the holiday season, each time I heard the song "Away In A Manger" I thought about what the woman had said in the Buffalo United Methodist Church the day of the boys' funeral.

Alex and Michael were also on the mind of a man from Florida. He came to South Carolina and planted a tall fir tree in the soil by John D. Long Lake and decorated it with Christmas ornaments in memory of Alex and Michael.

In February Doug Smith returned to Union to visit with his nephew David. Doug told me several times he felt David should go back to the media because he had been out of sight for such a long time. I told him, if David would agree to speak with me, the *Herald-Journal* would send the story to the Associated Press and throughout the *New York Times* newspaper chain.

On Saturday afternoon, February 4, 1995, David Smith decided to break his silence. About 4:30 p.m. Doug called my home and said, "David would like to talk with you for awhile. We'll drive up to Spartanburg."

"That's great," I told him. "I'll meet you in the newsroom." Before we hung up the telephone, I made certain Doug knew how to find the *Herald-Journal* building on West Main Street, and then tried to get myself fully awake. I didn't tell him, of course, but I was sound asleep when the telephone rang.

Bonner was at the newsroom when I arrived. He had just finished printing film from an earlier assignment and was about to leave for home. He stayed around when I told him what I was about to do. The photographer on duty could have worked with me on the interview but I was glad Bonner stayed. He and I had teamed on every interview the *Herald-Journal* had conducted with David and Susan.

I met David and Doug at the employee entrance. It was the first time I'd seen David in person for a long time. He was wearing a San Francisco 49ers jacket, a Christmas gift from his father. His face showed less strain and he smiled. We shook hands warmly and I invited him upstairs. David and Doug sat down on one side of a conference room table. Bonner and I sat across from them.

"I don't think my life could ever be normal – like it was – because I've lost my children," David said to me, as he sipped on a Coke. "That's not normal, and I can't go back to like it was."

David said he learned Susan had confessed to killing their children from a television news bulletin. He would not talk about his life with Susan before the tragedy that took his little boys' lives.

He did say this to me: "Susan changed four lives forever. The public needs to remember who the real victims were. Don't give up on Michael and Alex."

Then, without tears, David told me about the last time he saw his children alive. Grief was unable to deprive the young father of his smile as he remembered the Sunday afternoon he and his two little boys wrestled, read books and played with building blocks. This playtime with their dad was two days before Alex and Michael died in the dark waters of a Union County lake.

"Michael liked to have books read to him and Alex loved to stack up the blocks and then knock them over," David said. "They liked to wrestle, too. They were with me all Sunday afternoon and through the evening on October 23. We just did things dads like to do with their sons."

There were times during our conversation when David paused, so his voice would not break. Here was one of them:

> "I don't really have a good day. I have bad days and horrible days. I have to break it down to hour by hour, or minute by minute. Sometimes I find myself on my knees. It's not getting any easier. My comfort comes from relatives and close friends. They keep me going."

The deaths of his children were the second time David had faced the loss of a relative in three years. His 22-year-old brother, who was supposed to be best man at his and Susan's wedding, died of Crohns Disease 11 days before the ceremony. David's father filled the position.

In the months following Alex and Michael's deaths, mail poured into the Union, South Carolina post office from all over the world. The post office collected the cards and letters in long trays. Within three months after the boys' funeral they had handled more than 20,000 pieces of mail. Most of it was just addressed to "David Smith, Union, SC." Gifts came as well. A group of ten women sent a handmade quilt. The mail still comes.

"It's been very inspiring," David told me. "It's helped more than I could express to the public. To get a card that says, 'I'm thinking about you' or 'You are still in my prayers' is a boost that sometimes gets me to the next minute."

David went on to tell me how he tried to read every card and letter people had sent him. There was no doubt about what he would do with them.

"I will keep them forever," he said, smiling. "I treasure them."

It was dark when the two men left and headed back to Union. I went about my task of writing a story for the Sunday edition of the *Herald-Journal*. David Smith had broken his three-month silence. The story created a media fury. *The State* newspaper in Columbia, South Carolina ran the story on page one with David's photograph and my byline. While it was our "exclusive," the two newspapers have a reciprocal agreement and their editors were able to take the story off our computer. *Associated Press* asked for the story as well. They sent it nationwide.

On that same Sunday, a story I had researched for weeks ran on page one just below David's story. It was about a woman named Sue Logue, the first women to die in South Carolina's electric chair since the state started using it in 1912. Sue Logue died in 1943 for her role in a family feud that took the lives of eight people. Five were murdered and three died in South

Carolina's death house. If Susan Smith is convicted of killing her children, she could be the third woman in the state to die this way. During the last six months, Molly McDonough has written numerous stories about hearings Susan was required to attend. The one on January 16, 1995 brought tears to Susan Smith's eyes in the courtroom – and mixed reactions from people in Union. Sixteenth Circuit Solicitor Tommy Pope announced he would seek the death penalty for Susan Smith. David Bruck, Susan's lawyer from Columbia, upstaged Pope on January 15. He called a news conference and announced Pope's intentions. Bruck is a nationally known anti-death penalty lawyer.

"Only the Good Lord has got the right to judge," Marion Hawkins, a convenience store owner, told me after the announcement was made. "But people have to pay for what they have done. I wouldn't want to be sitting on the jury that has to make that decision."

A Charlotte, North Carolina man visiting John D. Long Lake felt differently.

"She deserves what those little children got," said Charles Henson, standing near the boat ramp. "I'm not vengeful, but when I think about that car and picture this – it's justified."

After the hearing ended, Linda Russell stood on the courthouse steps and pleaded on national television for mercy for her daughter.

"This has been hard for us," Russell told reporters. "Me and my family love Michael and Alex. We miss them. Susan loves them. She misses them. We miss Susan. We love her."

Susan Smith's family filled two rows of courtroom benches at the hearing. Her estranged husband David was not present.

After the news conference, I returned to the newsroom and called David Smith's father, C. David Smith, at his home in California. He'd missed Russell's statement on television. I told him about Pope's announcement and asked him how he felt.

"Susan should have thought about what she did," Mr. Smith said. "I resent her family for trying to get public sympathy for her. Alex and Michael are the victims. The focus should be put on them."

Mr. Smith became emotional as he continued speaking about his dead grandsons. He told me Michael adored his mother. He questioned how his daughter-in-law could drown her children.

"How could she watch her car do that?" the grieving man said. "Michael had to be calling for his mama."

The people of Union County are still trying to recover from the tragedy that shocked them to the core of their being. It will be a long time before they heal completely, if they ever do.

For months after Alex and Michael's funeral, several groups collected money to build a memorial to the little boys whose deaths touched so many lives. On a sunny spring day, a large group of people gathered to dedicate a large blue and yellow playground unit to their memory. A sign was unveiled that read: "This Unit Is Dedicated In Memory Of Michael and Alex Smith for the Preservation of Child Safety Across the Globe."

In early May I traveled to Union to participate in a PBS television documentary about the coverage the Susan Smith story received. Long-time Union resident Barbara Rippy stopped by in front of the courthouse to speak with me and meet the television crew.

"Union may never be the same again," Rippy said. "But we're good people and we'll go on with life."

When we finished taping, I got in my car and started back to Spartanburg. On the way, I drove along Toney Road by the house where Susan Smith used to live with her two little boys. All the blinds were closed and drapes were drawn. The toys I'd seen in the carport in October had been taken away. A child's wading pool was lying in the yard by a storage shed. I paused in front of

Epilogue

the house for a closer look, but only for a moment.

As I drove away I decided to take Highway 215 back to Spartanburg. This time there were no people standing in their yards to watch the funeral procession go by, and the blue and white bows had disappeared. There were no balloons.

When I reached Bogansville, I turned onto the road that leads to the cemetery and drove to Alex and Michael's grave. I was the only visitor there in the quiet Carolina countryside. As I stood looking at the fresh flowers that people continue to place on the grave, a warm breeze blew in from the west and raindrops fell from the heavens. It was time to go home.

Herald-Journal photo by Mike Bonner

Oh! call my brother back to me!
I cannot play alone;
The summer comes with flower and bee –
Where is my brother gone?

– Felicia Dorothea Hemans
The Child's First Grief

THE STORY
IN PHOTOGRAPHS

The photographs on the following pages tell Susan Smith's story in graphic detail. Photographers Mike Bonner and Gerry Pate have given the world images of the 23-year-old mother that both disturb and bring sadness to the hearts of people everywhere. From the first photograph of Susan as she left the sheriff's office the day after her children disappeared to the final image of the flowers on their grave, the photographs follow a remarkable, and often unbelieveable, journey through nine days in Union, South Carolina.

The author and publisher of *Nine Days In Union – The Search for Alex and Michael Smith* would like to express sincere appreciation to the photographers and news staff of the Spartanburg *Herald-Journal* for their permission to use these photographs.

At the first news conference in his office on October 26, 1994 Union County Sheriff Howard Wells shows the composite of the man Susan Smith said took her children.

News conferences were moved to the parking lot outside the sheriff's office when the number of reporters arriving in Union increased. Here, Sheriff Howard Wells is joined by Chief of the State Law Enforcement Division Robert Stewart, far right, and an unidentified investigator.

Lt. Jeff Lawson escorts Susan Smith from the Union County Courthouse late Wednesday, October 26. Smith reported her children were kidnapped the previous evening about 9 p.m. In this photo she was leaving the sheriff's office after her first full day of questioning.

David and Susan Smith talk about the disappearance of their children, 14-month-old Alex and 3-year-old Michael, during an interview less than two days after they were reported missing. This was the last interview either of them did for members of the print media during the search.

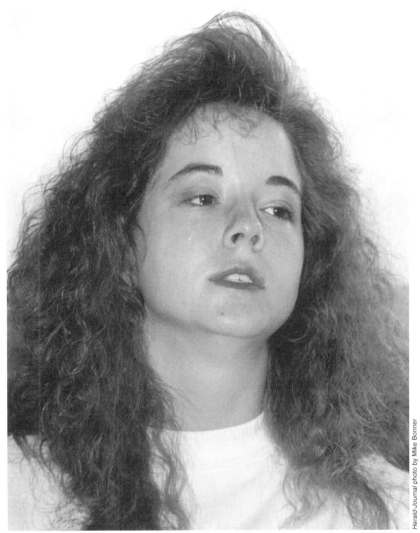

Herald-Journal photo by Mike Bonner

Susan Smith while talking with Gary Henderson in the living room of her mother's home Thursday morning, October 27, 1994. This photo was taken about 36 hours after she told police a black man took her children.

Photographs

Sheriff Howard Wells, on left, and other investigators leave a State Law
Enforcement Divison helicopter Wednesday morning, October 26, after
an air search of the woods surrounding John D. Long Lake.

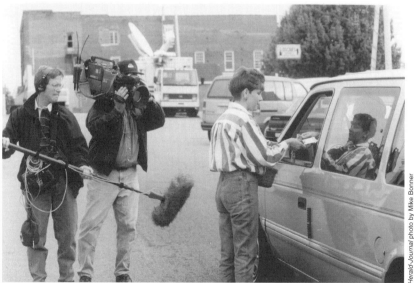

A television crew tapes an unidentified woman selling laminated photographs of the missing boys. The money raised from selling the photos
was donated to the Smiths.

Herald-Journal photo by Mike Bonner

David Smith makes an early plea for the return of his two children. Susan was not present when David made this plea on national television.

The intersection where Susan Smith said a black man jumped in her car is a short distance from downtown Union. Monarch Mill is in the background.

Local and national media converged on Union. WSPA-TV's Cynthia Barnes reports live from Union.

Herald-Journal photo by Mike Bonner

Satellite trucks lined both sides of Union's Main Street for the nine-day search. After the second day, a total of 15 trucks like these created a corridor for motorists driving along the street.

Herald-Journal photo by Mike Bonner

A self-portrait of *Herald-Journal* photographer Mike Bonner, taken in the middle of the night, while he camped in his van across the street from the Union County Courthouse.

Herald-Journal photo by Mike Bonner

Divers searched John D. Long Lake several times during the search for Alex and Michael. After Susan Smith confessed to killing the boys, she was able to give them information that helped locate her 1990 Mazda. The boys' bodies were found in their car seats in the rear seat of the car.

Margaret Gregory, who became David and Susan's spokeswoman for several days during the search, and Sheriff Howard Wells speak with reporters at a news conference.

Members of the media wait for a scheduled news conference.

Photographs

Union County citizens turned out in large numbers on Saturday, after the boys disappeared on Tuesday, to light candles and pray at the Bethel United Methodist Church. The church is located at the intersection where Susan told the police a man took her children.

Residents combed every section of Union County looking for any trace of Alex and Michael. These citizens searched wooded areas on horseback.

Gary Henderson

Herald-Journal photo by Mike Bonner

A mother and her child light candles and pray for Alex and Michael.

NBC News crew barbecue chicken on a new grill they bought at a Union discount store.

NBC News kept a large staff of reporters, producers and technicians in Union throughout the search and for several days after it was over.

Gary Henderson

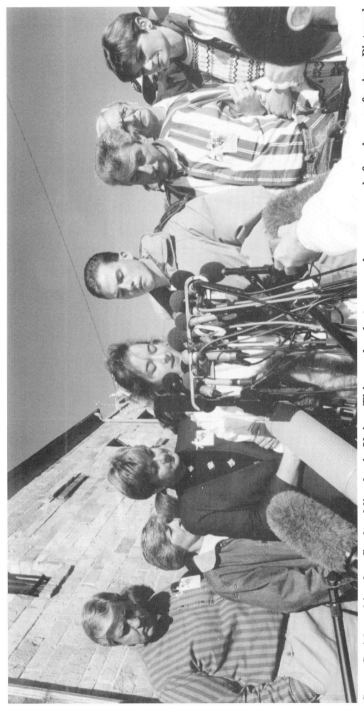

Herald-Journal photo by Gerry Pate

Susan Smith making her final public plea in Union. This was her last personal appearance before her confession. Pictured left to right are: Bev Russel, Linda Russell, Margaret Gregory, Susan V. Smith, David Smith, C. David Smith, Doug Smith and Susan Smith.

WYFF-TV news anchors Michael Cogdill and Carol Goldsmith interview Sheriff Howard Wells outside the Greenville, South Carolina television station's mobile studio.

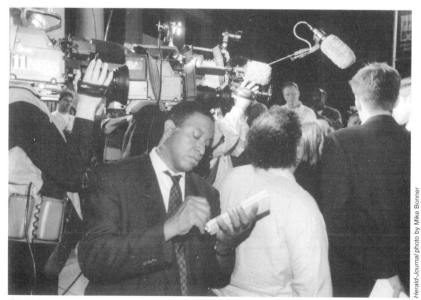

CBS News Correspondent Randall Pinkston prepares to go on the air with the story of Susan Smith's confession.

Herald-Journal photo by Mike Bonner

A man and woman parked near the entrance of John D. Long Lake listened to Union radio station WBCU while Sheriff Howard Wells read the statement announcing Susan Smith's confession.

Herald-Journal photo by Gerry Pate

Gilliam Edwards encouraged Union's black citizens to speak out moments after Susan Smith's confession was read.

Herald-Journal photo by Mike Bonner

Susan Smith's 1990 Mazda Protegé is hauled away after it was pulled from the bottom of John D. Long Lake on the night of November 3. Mud can be seen stuck to the right rear wheel. The car was found turned upside down and resting on its top by divers with the SC Department of Natural Resources.

Herald-Journal photo by Gerry Pate

Doug Smith became the Smith family spokesman after Susan confessed to drowning her little boys. Mr. Smith is David's uncle and lives in Michigan. He was in Union during most of the search period and stayed for about 10 days following Alex and Michael's funeral.

A member of Buffalo United Methodist Church puts the finishing touch on a display in the church lobby that was put up to honor the boys.

Oprah Winfrey talks with Kevin Kingsmore at a Saturday taping of her show at the Buffalo United Methodist Church. More than 300 people attended the taping of the show. Several other nationally televised shows originated from Union during the nine-day search period or shortly thereafter.

People started coming to Holcombe Funeral Home at 10 a.m. on Saturday for visitation. Here is a portion of the long line that stretched across the parking lot for hours. The families received condolences of the mourners for over three hours on Saturday night.

Sunday at 1 p.m. the single casket holding the bodies of Alex and Michael Smith is carried into the Buffalo United Methodist Church.

Herald-Journal photo by Mike Bonner

David Smith is supported by his uncle Doug Smith and his step-mother Susan Smith as he leaves Buffalo United Methodist Church after the funeral on Sunday afternoon, November 6.

Herald-Journal photo by Mike Bonner

David Smith turns for a final look at his little boys' casket as it is loaded into the rear of a hearse for the ride to Bogansville United Methodist Church Cemetery.

Herald-Journal photo by Mike Bonner

Flower arrangements covered a large area the day of the funeral. Six months after the little boys were buried, new flowers still appear on their grave regularly.

For months, John D. Long Lake has drawn the curious who want to see the place where the unspeakable crime was committed. It also draws those who still mourn. The children are standing at the spot where the car rolled into the water.

Flowers were scattered all along the shore at John D. Long Lake.

Peace.

Herald-Journal photo by Mike Bonner

Herald-Journal photo by Mike Bonner

The media and locals gather early on the day Susan Smith returned to the Union County Courthouse.

Herald-Journal photo by Mike Bonner

Susan Smith's parents, Bev and Linda Russell, arrive at the courthouse for their daughter's hearing. Mr. Russell later admitted he sexually molested Susan when she was a teenager.

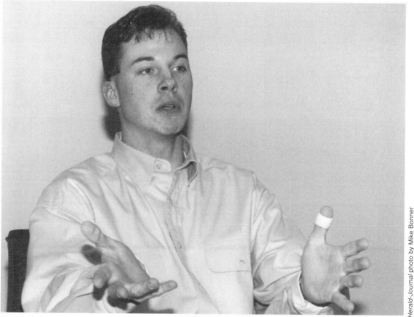

Herald-Journal photo by Mike Bonner

David Smith reacts to a question during a February 4, 1995 interview. It was the first time David had spoken to a member of the press for more than three months.

Herald-Journal photo by Mike Bonner

Herald-Journal photo by Mike Bonner

Looking a lot less stressfull, David Smith reflects on happier times with his children.

Sixteenth Circuit Solicitor Tommy Pope announced he will seek the death penalty for Susan Smith.

THIS UNIT IS DEDICATED
IN THE MEMORY OF
MICHAEL & ALEX SMITH
FOR THE PRESERVATION
OF CHILD SAFETY
ACROSS THE GLOBE

Herald-Journal photo by Mike Bonner

David Smith looks over a playground unit at a park in Union that was dedicated to his children five months after their deaths.

When I left my home on Tuesday, October 25, I was very emotionally distraught. I didn't want to live anymore! I felt like things could never get any worse. When I left home, I was going to ride around a little while and then go to my mom's. As I rode and rode and rode, I felt even more anxiety coming upon me about not wanting to live. I felt I couldn't be a good mom anymore but I didn't want my children to grow up without a mom. I felt I had to end our lives to protect us all from any grief or harm. ~~xxxxxxxxxxxxxxxxxx~~ I had never felt so lonely and so sad in my entire life. I was in <u>love</u> with someone very much, but he didn't love me and never would. I had a very difficult time accepting that. And I had hurt him very much and I could see why he could never love me. When I was @ John D. Long Lake, ~~xxxxxxxx~~ I had never felt so scared and unsure as I did when I wanted to end my life so bad and was in my car ready to go down that ramp into the water and I did go part way, but it stopped. I went again and stopped. I then got out of the car and ~~xxx~~ stood by the car a nervous wreck. Why was I feeling this way? Why was everything so bad in my life? I had no answers to these questions. I dropped to the lowest when I allowed my children to go down that ramp into the water without me. I took off running and screaming "Oh God! Oh God, NO!" What have I done? Why did you let this happen? I wanted to turn around so bad and go back, but I knew it was too late. I was an absolute mental case! I couldn't believe what I had done. I love my children w/ all my ♥. That will never change. I have prayed to them for forgiveness and hope that they will find it in their ♥ to forgive me. I never

117

meant to hurt them!! I am SORRY for what has happened and I know what I need some help. I don't think I will ever be able to forgive myself for what I have done. My children, Michael and Alex, are with our Heavenly Father now and I know that they will never be hurt again. As a mom, that means more than words could ever say.

I knew from day one, the truth would prevail, but I was so scared. I didn't know what to do. It was very tough emotionally to sit and watch my family hurt like they did. It was time to bring a peace of mind to everyone, including myself. My children deserve to have the best and now they will. I broke down on Thursday, November 3 and told Sheriff Howard Wells the truth. It wasn't easy, but after the truth was out, I felt like the world was lifted off my shoulders. I know now that it is going to be a tough and long road ahead of me. At this very moment, I don't feel I will be able to handle what's coming, but I have prayed to God that he give me the strength to survive each day and to face these times and situations in my life that will be extremely painful. I have put my total faith in God and He will take care of me.

Susan V. Smith
11/3/94
5:05 p.m.

WITNESS
Cary D. Allison, FBI, Greenville, S.C.
Jansing Regan, SLED, Cola. S.C.

ARREST WARRANT

D- 893269

STATE OF SOUTH CAROLINA
☒ County/ ☐ Municipality of
UNION

THE STATE
against

Susan Smith

Address: _____

Phone: _____ SSN: _____
Sex: F Race: W Height: _____ Weight: _____
DL State: _____ DL#: _____
DOB: _____ Agency ORI#: _____
Prosecuting Agency: UCSO
Prosecuting Officer: W. Howard Wells
Offense: Murder
Code/Ordinance Sec: 16-3-10 Offense Code: _____

This warrant is CERTIFIED FOR SERVICE in the ☐ County/ ☐ Municipality of _____. The accused is to be arrested and brought before me to be dealt with according to law.

_____ (L.S.)
Signature of Judge

Date _____

RETURN

A copy of this arrest warrant was delivered to defendant on _____

_____
Signature of Constable/Law Enforcement Officer

RETURN WARRANT TO: _____

Form Approved by
S.C. Attorney General
July 26, 1960
SCCA 518

AFFIDAVIT

STATE OF SOUTH CAROLINA)
☒ County/ ☐ Municipality of)
UNION

Personally appeared before me the affiant W. Howard Wells, Sheriff being duly sworn deposes and says that defendant Susan Smith did within this county and state on /about October 25, 1994 violate the criminal laws of th... State of South Carolina (or ordinance of ☐ County/ ☐ Municipality of _____ in the following particulars:
DESCRIPTION OF OFFENSE: Murder

I further state that there is probable cause to believe that the defendant named above did commit the crime set forth and that probable cause is based on the following facts:

did commit the crime of Murder in that Susan Smith did, in Union County, willfully and unlawfully and with malice aforethought kill one, Alexander Tyler Smith; in violation of SEction 16-3-10 of the S.C. Code of Laws 1976 as amended in such case made and provided. Probable cause being based on a confession by the defendant.

_____
Signature of Affiant
Affiant's Address _____
Affiant's Telephone _____

Sworn to and subscribed before me
on November 3, 1994 (L.S.)
_____
Signature of Issuing Judge

ARREST WARRANT

STATE OF SOUTH CAROLINA)
☒ County/ ☐ Municipality of)
Union

TO ANY LAW ENFORCEMENT OFFICER OF THIS STATE OR MUNICIPALITY OR ANY CONSTABLE OF THIS COUNTY:
It appearing from the above affidavit that there are reasonable grounds to believe that defendant Susan Smith did violate the criminal laws of the State of South Carolina (or ordinance of ☐ County/ ☐ Municipality of _____) as set forth below:
DESCRIPTION OF OFFENSE: Murder

Now, therefore, you are empowered and directed to arrest the said defendant and bring him or her before me forthwith to be dealt with according to law. A copy of this Arrest Warrant shall be delivered to the defendant at the time of its execution, or as soon thereafter as is practicable.

_____ (L.S.)
Signature of Issuing Judge
Judge Code: 491
Judge's Address Union County Courthouse PO Box 200 Union, S.C. 29379
Judge's Telephone 429 1648
Issuing Court ☒ Magistrate ☐ Municipal ☐ Circuit

ORIGINAL

Form Approved by
S.C. Attorney General
July 7th 1980
SCCA 518

ARREST WARRANT

D- 893268

STATE OF SOUTH CAROLINA
☒ County/☐ Municipality of
Union

THE STATE
against

Susan Smith
Address: 407 Toney Road
Union, S.C. 29379
Phone: _____ SSN: _____
Sex: F Race: W Height: 5-3 Weight: 130
DL State: _____ DL #: _____
DOB: _____ Agency ORI #: _____
Prosecuting Agency: UCSO
Prosecuting Officer: W. Howard Wells
Offense: Murder
Code/Ordinance Sec: 16-3-10 Offense Code: _____

This warrant is CERTIFIED FOR SERVICE in the
☐ County/☐ Municipality of _____ The accused
is to be arrested and brought before me to be
dealt with according to law.

_____ (L.S.)
Signature of Judge

Date: _____

RETURN
A copy of this arrest warrant was delivered to
defendant _____
on _____

_____
Signature of Constable/Law Enforcement Officer

RETURN WARRANT TO:

STATE OF SOUTH CAROLINA)
☒ County/☐ Municipality of)
Union)

AFFIDAVIT

Personally appeared before me the affiant W. Howard Wells,Sheriff who
being duly sworn deposes and says that defendant Susan Smith
did within this county and state on/about October 25, 1994 violate the criminal laws of the
State of South Carolina (or ordinance of ☐ County/☐ Municipality of _____)
in the following particulars:
DESCRIPTION OF OFFENSE: Murder

I further state that there is probable cause to believe that the defendant named above did commit
the crime set forth and that probable cause is based on the following facts:

did commit the crime of Murder in that Susan Smith did, in Union County,
wilfully and unlawfully and with malice aforethought kill one, Michael
Daniel Smith; in violation of Section 16-3-10 of the S.C. Code of Laws, 1976
as amended in such case made and provided.
Probable cause being based on a confession by the defendant.

Sworn to and subscribed before me
on November 3, 1994)
) (L.S.)
_____
Signature of Issuing Judge

_____
Signature of Affiant

Affiant's Address: _____

Affiant's Telephone: _____

ARREST WARRANT

STATE OF SOUTH CAROLINA)
☒ County/☐ Municipality of)
Union)

TO ANY LAW ENFORCEMENT OFFICER OF THIS STATE OR MUNICIPALITY OR ANY CONSTABLE OF THIS COUNTY:
It appearing from the above affidavit that there are reasonable grounds to believe that
defendant Susan Smith
on/about October 25, 1994 did violate the criminal laws of the State of South Carolina (or ordinance of
☐ County/☐ Municipality of _____) as set forth below.
DESCRIPTION OF OFFENSE: Murder

Now, therefore, you are empowered and directed to arrest the said defendant and bring him or her before
me forthwith to be dealt with according to law. A copy of this Arrest Warrant shall be delivered to the
defendant at the time of its execution, or as soon thereafter as is practicable.

_____ (L.S.)
Signature of Issuing Judge

Judge Code: 497

Judge's Address: Union County Courthouse
PO Box 200 Union, S.C. 29379
Judge's Telephone: 429 1648
Issuing Court: ☒ Magistrate ☐ Municipal ☐ Circuit

ORIGINAL

ARTICLES

Herald-Journal, Spartanburg, South Carolina
Thursday, October 27, 1994

A Mother's frantic call: "I love y'all"
Children's Kidnapper still eludes authorities

By Gary Henderson
Staff Writer

UNION - Susan Smith said she stood in the middle of a rural highway Tuesday night and screamed "I love y'all" as a stranger drove into the darkness with her two screaming children.

The boys, ages 14 months and 3 years, and their abductor have not been seen since that time, despite a nationwide manhunt that included helicopter searches on Wednesday.

Mrs. Smith, 23, said her nightmare began Tuesday about 9:15 p.m., when she stopped for a traffic signal in the Monarch Mill community. A man with a handgun jumped into the passenger seat of her burgundy 1990 Mazda Protegé.

"I was looking out the left window, and the man opened the door and got in," Mrs Smith said. "When I asked him what he wanted, he said, 'Shut up and drive or I'll kill you.'"

Mrs. Smith said her children began to cry, and 3-year-old Michael said, "Who is this man, Mommy?"

Mrs. Smith said she didn't know the man, and she believes he chose her car at random. He was out of breath, as though he had been running, when he jumped in, she said.

At the abductor's direction, she drove northwest of Union for about 10 miles. Then the man suddenly told her to stop the car. Mrs. Smith said she asked if she should pull over, but the man said for her stop in the middle of the road.

Then he ordered her to get out of the car.

"I begged him to let me keep my children," Mrs. Smith said. "But he said, 'I don't have time, I'll take care of them.'"

The man pushed her onto Highway 49 near John D. Long Lake, Mrs. Smith said, and he drove away as both children cried for their mother.

"I stood in the middle of the road and screamed, 'I love y'all,'" Mrs. Smith said. "And when he was gone, I ran to a house for help."

The Union County Sheriff's Office arrived a few minutes later, and an all-points bulletin was issued for the car by 10 p.m.

Mrs. Smith was taken to her parents' home in Union, where the family gathered Wednesday to wait for word about the search.

The boys' father, 24-year-old David Smith, fought back tears as he talked about his missing children. Mr. Smith, the assistant manager of a Winn-Dixie Store in Union, said he was at work when he learned his children had been abducted.

"I thought I was going out of my mind as I drove over there," Mr. Smith said. "I didn't know how to react."

The young father said Wednesday morning that he had not slept since the children disappeared. He said he can only think about his two young boys.

"Everywhere I look, I see their play toys and pictures," Mr. Smith said. "They are both wonderful children. I don't know how else to put it. And I can't imagine life without them."

Dozens of law enforcement officers converged on Union Wednesday, and friends and neighbors helped to search the area for the two boys.

Mrs. Smith said Union County sheriff's investigators and agents for the State Law Enforcement Division questioned her for about six hours Wednesday, asking her to repeat details about the kidnapping.

Investigators apologized for asking her probing questions, she said, but they told her they had to cover every possible angle in their investigation. Mrs. Smith said she assured them that she understood.

"I told them I would never hurt my children. I've been heart-broken by this."

Appendix

Herald-Journal, Spartanburg, South Carolina
Thursday, October 27, 1994

Union County residents rally to search for kidnapper

By Gary Henderson
Staff Writer

UNION - As word spread Wednesday of the abduction of two toddlers, the people of Union County formed private search parties and prayer chains in hopes that the children would be found safe.

The Tuesday night carjacking and kidnapping of the two youngsters from their mother frightened residents in this county of 31,000.

"This makes me scared," said Susie Bridges, 46, from her car near the law enforcement command post at the county courthouse Wednesday. "Nothing like this has ever happened in Union County."

Susan Smith, 23, told police Tuesday that a man jumped into her car at a traffic light near Monarch Mills and ordered her to drive away. About 10 miles down the road, Smith said the man ordered her out of the car and sped away with her two children.

Police immediately launched a massive search for 14-month-old Alexander Smith and his brother, 3-year-old Michael.

But the children had not been found by late Wednesday.

The little boys' mother and father, relatives and friends gathered to wait for information about the search at the home of the boys' grandparents, Bev and Linda Russell.

While the family waited, their friends and neighbors got in their cars and drove all over the Upstate and into North Carolina, looking for any sign of the missing children. Others searched on foot in the area near John D. Long Lake where the children disappeared.

"I was out looking all night, and I'll be going back out again,"

Walt Garner said. "If I'm just standing around, I feel helpless."

Garner said his daughter, Donna, and the boys' mother have been friends since they were small children.

"I was holding these two children in my lap Monday night," Garner said as tears flowed down his face. Overcome with emotion, he couldn't say any more.

"I don't know why he didn't give her them babies," Garner's friend, Scott Silver, said of the kidnapper. "These are not rich people. There's no ransom or anything in it for him – nothing but trouble."

By 10 a.m. Wednesday, satellite trucks from seven television stations and reporters from newspapers all over the Carolinas had converged on the Union County Courthouse.

At a Wednesday afternoon news conference, Union County Sheriff Howard Wells said his office had received calls from the major television networks and the television show America's Most Wanted.

As reporters and photographers moved through the community Wednesday, citizens often stopped them to ask whether the children had been spotted.

Bystanders also clustered along the sidewalk in front of the courthouse and watched the army of local, state and federal officers come and go from the command center.

Kevin Kingsmore, a 23-year-old graphic artist from Union, worked throughout the morning to design a flier that he said would be handed out by volunteers all over the Upstate.

"I've been out looking all afternoon," said 27-year-old Wendy Fowler, holding a stack of Kingsmore's fliers. "I'm doing everything I can. I've prayed for these children all day."

Herald-Journal, Spartanburg, South Carolina
Friday, October 28, 1994

Nation searches for 2 little boys
N.C. robbery may offer clue to kidnapper

By Gary Henderson
Staff Writer

UNION - After two days of the most intense police investigation in Union County history, police are no closer to learning who abducted two small children during a carjacking earlier this week.

There's not one new lead.

"In 20 years of law enforcement, I've never worked a case that had so little to work with," said Union County Sheriff Howard Wells. "But there's not any more that can be done."

Meanwhile, the story of the young mother and the abduction of her sons, 3 years and 14 months old, has become the talk of the nation with almost every major news organization airing stories Thursday.

Thursday afternoon, the boys' father, David Smith, used the national media to make a passionate plea for the return of his sons.

"I plead with the man to return our children safe and sound," Mr. Smith said to the hoard of reporters assembled outside the court house. "It gets harder as time goes by to deal with this."

Smith ended his plea to the abductor by saying his 14-month-old needed a bottle before he goes to bed at night.

Susan Smith, 23, of Toney Road, in Union, said a man carjacked her 1990 burgundy Mazda Protegé at a Monarch Mills intersection about 9:15 Tuesday evening. She said the man forced her to drive about five miles northeast of Union, and then forced her out of the car near John D. Long Lake. He then took off with Smith's sons, 3-year-old Michael and his brother, Alexander Smith.

Gary Henderson

Herald-Journal, Spartanburg, South Carolina
Friday, October 28, 1994

Yellow ribbons fly for Union children

By Gary Henderson
Staff Writer

UNION- Yellow ribbons were tied to trees, telephone poles and doors and worn in lapels Thursday, as the people of Union County remembered two little boys.

"I've never experienced anything like this. I feel like they are my own," said Pat Gibson, as she placed a big yellow ribbon on her front door. "I'm keeping this up until the children come home."

Three-year-old Michael Smith and his brother, 14-month-old Alexander, have not been seen since about 9:15 p.m. Tuesday. Their mother, Susan Smith, 23, said they were abducted by a man that jumped into her car at a traffic light in Monarch Mills.

"All I can do now is trust in the Lord and my family," said Mrs. Smith from her parents' home Thursday morning. "I keep trying not to lose hope, but the more time passes, I get scared."

The mother of the two missing boys paused to gain her composure.

"If they are lying somewhere dead, I want them home," Mrs. Smith said. "Oh, God. I can't bear to think of that."

Mrs. Smith said when the man drove off with her children, she fell to the ground in despair.

"I started running down the middle of the road screaming, "Somebody's got my children."

Mrs. Smith said when she got to a nearby house, the people brought her inside and called the police.

"The woman kept telling me, 'Everything will be okay,' Mrs.

Smith said. "She put her arms around me and held me."

While Mrs. Smith and her husband, David, 24, talked about the disappearance of their children, the ribbons continued to go up on Main Street.

"I volunteered for this," said Daniel Glenn, a Union High School senior. "I thing it's bad to do something like that. It has been a shock for everybody here."

As Glenn spoke, he tied a yellow ribbon on a holly tree covered with red berries. It was one of 32 ribbons the young man placed on trees in downtown Union Thursday morning.

"I hope this is sending a message, letting everybody know how serious a problem it is," Glenn said. "And I hope I'm doing my part."

While some people hung yellow ribbons, others were thinking about the financial needs the Smith family will face.

Twenty-one-year-old Karen Harger and Audrey Roberts, 26, collected money to help the Smiths with expenses.

"I feel sorry for them," Roberts said. "Their bills won't stop, and they can't work right now."

Support for the Smiths in Union was expressed in other ways too. A sign on North Main Street read: "To David, Susan, Alexander, and Michael Smith – You are in our prayers."

The Smiths said the concern shown by other people has helped give them hope for the future.

"I have a lot of hope," Mrs. Smith said. "That's all I have. I can't imagine life without my children."

Thursday morning, police closed the roads leading to the lake while divers searched the area.

"I'm confident the car is not in the lake," Wells said. "We did it to rule out any evidence that we might have overlooked there."

Wells said investigators have interviewed at least 25 potential suspects.

"We're not ruling out anybody, including the parents," Wells said.

Susan Smith and her 24-year-old husband, David, spent the last two days being interviewed by Union County sheriff's officers. Wells would not say if the parents had taken a polygraph test.

According to records at the Union County Courthouse, Susan Smith filed for divorce from her husband on September 22. She listed adultery as the reason for wanting a divorce.

Mr. Smith declined to answer questions about his relationship with his wife.

But Wells said he didn't believe a domestic dispute was the reason for the boy's disappearance.

Wells said investigators are working 24 hours a day to develop a suspect list from information on known violent offenders. He said information about the abduction was given to a national police computer network shortly after the children were taken from their mother.

"We've received offers for help from all over the United States," Wells said. "Police from several areas of South Carolina have offered to provide manpower."

Wells said a behavior specialist is also being used to develop a profile of the the individual who abducted the children.

Margaret Frierson, executive director of the Adam Walsh Center in Columbia, said her organization is assisting the family by getting out fliers and photographs of the children.

She said about 112 children had been reported missing this year in South Carolina. Frierson said most of them had been either runaways or family abduction – but never a carjacking.

"I never experienced anything like this before," Frierson said.

Wells said he welcomes the national attention, which could help solve the case. He appeared on NBC's Today Show Thursday morning and CNN's Larry King Live Thursday night.

"I hope the suspect will see this and notify us where to pick the children up," Wells said.

The sheriff said more than 1,000 calls offering information have been received at the Union command center since the search began Tuesday night. Additional phone lines were installed at the Union County Courthouse Wednesday to handle the huge volume of calls.

"We are waiting for that call that will tell us where the children are located," Wells said Wednesday afternoon. "We've had reports of many sightings, but none that are credible, so far."

Officials have ruled out a reported sighting of the car in Greenville.

Wells said sightings have been called in from as far away as upstate New York.

"We'll be looking in every direction," Wells said.

Herald-Journal, Spartanburg, South Carolina
Saturday, October 29, 1994

'We are not ruling out anything'
Children pray for playmates

By Gary Henderson
Staff Writer

UNION - As area law enforcement launched a massive search for two little boys, the children in Judy Cathcart's care knelt by a sofa and prayed: "Help this man bring Michael and Alexander back to play with us."

But the boys, 3-year-old Michael Smith and his 14-month-old brother, Alexander, have not returned.

And so, Cathcart and the parents of the boys' day-care playmates have had the task of explaining why Michael and Alexander are missing.

The morning after the boys' disappearance was perhaps the toughest.

"It was tearful," Cathcart said, "When the mothers dropped off their children Wednesday morning."

After the mothers left, Cathcart talked to the children and tried to explain what had happened to Michael and Alexander.

"The children asked if they could pray for the boys," said Cathcart, her voice choking. "I asked if they'd like to hold hands while we prayed. But they said, 'Can we get on our knees?'"

Cathcart, who cares for children in her home, has known the boys' mother, Susan Smith, all her life and had baby-sat for the boys since they were infants.

Michael and Alexander were regulars at the home of Cathcart and her husband, Carol. The boys were there Tuesday, the day they were abducted along with their mother's burgundy Mazda Protegé near Monarch Mill.

A man, armed with a gun, jumped into Mrs. Smith's car and forced the 23-year-old Union woman to drive a few miles on Highway 49 before making her get out of the car and driving off with the boys.

"The children (at the day-care center) knew all about it," Mrs. Cathcart said. "Their parents had talked to them and told them Michael and Alexander wouldn't be here."

Cathcart said there's nothing sweeter – or sadder – than a child's prayer for a playmate.

"They all knelt in front of the sofa, and each one of them said a little prayer," Cathcart said. "But we had to stop a few times to dry away the tears."

Cathcart said one 5-year-old boy prayed this way:

"God, please help Alex and Michael. I hope the man has it in his heart to bring them back."

The families whose children stay in Cathcart's home each day are close to one another. The children have grown up together, Cathcart said, and they sometimes behave like brothers and sisters.

"One of my 2-year-olds didn't want to start lunch one day," Cathcart said. "She said, 'We can't eat until Michael and Alexander get here. They're just late.'"

Cathcart said when the parents come to pick up their children each day, they usually visit with one another.

Now, many are wearing a small yellow ribbon and a laminated photograph of Michael and Alexander.

On Thursday, the children in Cathcart's care hung two yellow ribbons – one for each of the boys – on a tree in front of Cathcart's home.

"All this week I've been trying to tell the children things they should do to be safe, you know, like stay with their mommy," Cathcart said.

But Cathcart, who has two grown children herself, said one little boy gave her a grim reminder.

He said, "Michael and Alexander were with their mommy, when something happened to them."

Herald-Journal, Spartanburg, South Carolina
Tuesday, November 1, 1994

It was still Halloween in Union

By Gary Henderson
Staff Writer

UNION - Hundreds of children in Halloween costumes put a smile back on the face of downtown Union Monday afternoon. The youngsters descended on stores and businesses for more than an hour in the downtown merchants' annual trick or treat outing for children.

"These children have to go on, they can't continue to be sad," said Mamie McBeth. "They have to feel like children, but they just have to be more careful."

McBeth taught third grade at Jonesville Elementary School for more than 30 years. Now, she works part time at the Union County Schools Parents Resource Center on Main Street. When McBeth recognized former students in the crowd Monday afternoon, they got a handful of candy, a warm greeting and a hug.

The retired school teacher said the abduction a week ago of 3-year-old Michael Smith and his 14-month-old brother, Alexander, has weighed heavily on her and other town residents.

"We are still praying and thinking about the little children, but at the same time, we have to get on with our lives," McBeth said.

Outside Greene's Salvage, employees handed out full-sized bags of candy.

"We don't know how many we'll have come by," said store owner, Alan Greene. "But we have enough candy for about 3,000 kids."

Greene said he liked the idea of having the kids downtown for trick or treating, because it offers them a safe place to go.

"Kids don't always understand why you can't go out just any-where and have fun," Greene said. Steve Smith, 13, a sixth-grader at Excelsior Middle School, stopped to check out the bag of treats he'd received along the street.

"I'm trying to get this full," the young boy said, taking stock of his inventory. He moved on to the next business with his huge shopping bag.

As children filled Union's downtown sidewalks Monday after-noon, so did the news media. Television crews and reporters mixed with young trick or treaters from the courthouse to the north end of Main Street.

CBS News correspondent Elizabeth Kaledin finished a report for the network's Seattle affiliate, and then began handing out more than news. She gave every child that passed the CBS truck a handful of Reese's Peanut Butter Cups.

Engineers decorated the large van with black and orange stream-ers. A sign on the side of the truck read: "Trick or treaters welcome."

Kaledin said the media are not always well-received when they swoop into an area, but she said Union has been different.

"The people of Union have been wonderful," Kaledin said. "They brought in the chicken biscuits for lunch today. It was delicious. We are paying back their wonderful hospitality."

On the north end of Main Street, 22-year-old Lesley Austin watched her children as they went door to door collecting treats.

"You can't just focus on this all the time," Austin said of the abduction. "The children are having fun and it's not that we don't care. But life can't stop in Union. We have to go on."

Appendix

Herald-Journal, Spartanburg, South Carolina
Thursday, November 3, 1994

Klaas says family making mistake by not talking

By Gary Henderson
Staff Writer

The father of Polly Klaas, whose kidnapping from her California home last year captured national attention, says David and Susan Smith of Union are making a mistake by not being more open with the news media.

Marc Klaas, now a journalist with the television show "American Journal", said he told the family's spokeswoman, Margaret Gregory, that he would like to visit with the Smiths without cameras or microphones.

"I tried to make it clear what I wanted to do," Klaas said. "I wanted to talk with them parent to parent."

But Klaas said he believes Gregory kept him from talking to the Smiths.

"After four days, I gave up and went home," Klaas said from California Wednesday morning.

"They said the parents were suffering too much grief to talk to anybody," Klaas said. "I tried really hard for four days, but they didn't want to talk to me."

Klaas' 12-year-old daughter, Polly, was abducted from home last October in a case that attracted nationwide attention. Polly had friends over for a slumber party when a man walked through the door and grabbed her. Polly's slain body was found about two months later under a stack of plywood 50 miles from home.

The Smiths granted reporters interviews the first two days after their children disappeared, but Gregory said they stopped because they needed time with their family.

Gregory, a former journalist, handles public relations for the Richland County Sheriff's Department in Columbia.

"I am a family member, and my department allowed me to take vacation on short notice," Gregory said. "David and Susan needed time for themselves to gather their thoughts. They were overwhelmed. That's why they asked me to handle it for them."

The Smiths made a tearful appeal Wednesday morning for the safe return of their children. It was the first public appearance for the couple in several days. They did not take questions from reporters after their statements.

John Rabon, vice president of the National Center for Missing and Exploited Children in Arlington, Virginia, said the likelihood the children have been harmed increases the longer the ordeal drags on.

"It increases by the minute," Rabon said. "It is not a good situation, considering the tender age of the kids."

Rabon said without a car and witnesses other than the children's mother, the case seems hopeless. He said prior cases like this one cannot be studied because there are none.

Rabon said the lack of clues makes it ever important to keep abduction of the Smith children alive in the news media.

"This case is like Jell-O." Rabon said. "The more you squeeze it, the less you have in your hand.

"Why would a black man steal two white children?"

Rabon said officials have reached an unpleasant point in the investigation.

"You've got to start looking at family members and friends," Rabon said. "They'll have to receive more investigation than before."

Klaas said he wanted to let the Smiths know how law enforcement agencies look at the abduction of children.

"It was important for them to know parents are the No. 1 suspects," Klaas said. "About 98 percent of all abductions of children are committed by family members. It's rare for a child to be abducted by a stranger."

Officials have not identified any family members as suspects.

Klaas said when his daughter disappeared from her home, he told police he'd do anything necessary to eliminate himself as a suspect so they could turn their attention to an unknown abductor.

A prison parolee was later arrested and charged with Polly's murder.

Herald-Journal, Spartanburg, South Carolina
Friday, November 4, 1994

Mother confesses; two boys are dead
Bodies still in car pulled from John D. Long Lake

By Gary Henderson and Reginald Fields
Staff Writers

UNION - Nine days after a Union woman said she stood in the middle of a dark highway and watched a man drive away with her screaming children, Susan V. Smith confessed to killing them.

Sources say that police have questioned a man said to be Smith's boyfriend who is wealthy and didn't want the children.

Investigators declined to comment on a motive after the arrest Thursday.

Smith, 23, of 407 Toney Road, was arrested by sheriff's deputies late Thursday afternoon. She is being held at the York County Detention Center and is scheduled to be arraigned in court at 11 a.m. today in Union.

York Jail Lt. Ted Melton said Smith would be watched closely for her own safety.

"We will have to isolate her," Melton said. "Because of all the stress in this case, she might be suicidal or something."

Sixteenth Circuit Solicitor Tommy Pope said a mental evaluation for Smith is a possibility.

State Law Enforcement Division spokesman Hugh Munn said Thursday no further arrests are expected in the murders of the two Smith children.

Munn said Smith told investigators early in the afternoon the car could be found in John D. Long Lake, 7 miles northeast of Union.

Union County Sheriff Howard Wells said Smith's burgundy

135

Mazda Protegé was found submerged just off a boat ramp. Two small bodies were found in the back seat of the car. Munn said investigators believe those to be the bodies of Michael Smith, 3, and his 14-month-old brother, Alexander Smith.

Autopsies will be performed this morning to make a positive identification.

"I'm not going to say I was surprised or shocked," Wells said. "We knew from the very start what the possible scenario would be."

Investigators had searched John D. Long Lake several times, but did not find the car.

"This could easily happen when the lake is muddy," Munn said. "It's a big lake, and it was not easy to pinpoint."

Munn said divers from the South Carolina Department of Natural Resources found the car about sundown. He said divers used lights to determine it was the missing car and that two bodies were in the back seat.

Smith was detained about 2 p.m. Thursday and divers found the car several hours later, Munn said.

On Thursday evening about 6 p.m. Wells and SLED Chief Robert Stewart flew by helicopter to the home of Smith's parents, Bev and Linda Russell, in the Mount Vernon Estates section of Union. Wells and Stewart told the Russells their daughter was being charged with the murders of their grandchildren.

Less than an hour later, Wells announced the arrest to a throng of reporters and townspeople, who had heard word of a major development.

"Susan Smith has been arrested and charged with two counts of murder in connection with her children Michael, 3, and Alexander, 14 months," Wells said.

A large gasp rose from the crowd.

Although authorities declined to say what they believe the motive is, CNN reported Thursday night that police have a letter from Smith's boyfriend saying he did not want a ready-made family. The boyfriend was described by sources as a wealthy man and is not Mitch Sinclair, who had been identified earlier as a friend of Smith's.

"I can't believe she killed her children," said Annette Phillips of

Union. "That woman hurt a lot of people."

The children's grandmother, Barbara Benson of Garden City, said her son, David, was shattered by the news.

"No, he's not OK," Ms. Benson said of her son's condition. "He's locked in a room and he won't even talk to his father.

"Nobody knows why, I mean nobody knows the motive, I guess."

Munn said officials began to doubt a carjacking had taken place early in the investigation because of inconsistencies in Smith's statements.

"After a time when the vehicle was not spotted, it did not meet the classic definition of a carjacking," Munn said.

Smith told Union County deputies a black man jumped into her car near Monarch Mill about 9:15 p.m. on Oct. 25. She said the man forced her to drive at gunpoint along Highway 49, made her get out of the car near John D. Long Lake and then drove away with her two children still in the car.

Smith knocked on the door of the house near the lake entrance about 10 p.m. and said her children had been taken.

A massive search to locate the boys was launched by Union County sheriff's officers, the FBI and SLED agents. The story attracted the major news media from across the country.

"I think the press attention to this case was very beneficial," Wells said. "The national attention, the intense pressure, the scrutiny by the media probably had a great deal to do with this case being broken."

During the nine-day search Smith and her husband, David, made several tearful and impassioned pleas on national television for the safe return of their children.

While Mrs. Smith was being held, family spokeswoman Margaret Gregory was answering reporters' questions at the Russell home.

She said that Mrs. Smith was hurt that people thought she would harm her children but that she understood why the focus had shifted to her.

The National Center for Missing and Exploited Children and The Adam Walsh Foundation expanded the search for the missing boys nationwide. Thousands of tips poured in from all over the country.

Rumors that a major announcement would be made at a 5:30 p.m.

news conference spread quickly throughout Union County on Thursday afternoon. A crowd of several hundred people gathered outside the courthouse to hear Wells read the brief statement saying Mrs. Smith was charged with the murders of her children.

When the news conference ended, police had to block Main Street because of the milling crowd.

Staff Writer Shelly Haskins contributed to this report.

Herald-Journal, Spartanburg, South Carolina
Saturday, November 5, 1994

'Hideous' scene ended ordeal
Crowd jeers as mother goes to court

By Gary Henderson
Staff Writer

On Oct. 25, Susan V. Smith placed her two young sons in their car seats and drove northeast along Highway 49 to the east entrance of Union County's John D. Long Lake. The 23-year-old mother got out of the car, put it in drive and allowed her 1990 Mazda Protegé to roll down a boat ramp into the cold, dark waters.

Her sons – 3-year-old Michael and 14-month-old Alex – were alive and buckled into their seats as the car floated on the lake, rolled over and sank.

"It was hideous," said an investigator who was on the scene Thursday night, when the car was dragged from the lake. "There were people crying everywhere. Police officers were crying."

The scene was the end of a 10-day nationwide search for the little boys, an ordeal that started when Smith told police a black man carjacked her vehicle, forced her to drive a few miles and then made her get out of her car without her children.

While officials will not discuss a motive, speculation has surrounded a letter from Smith's former boyfriend, Tom Findlay, whose family runs Conso Products, where Smith worked. In the letter, Findlay said he was not ready for a family.

A Conso spokeswoman released a statement Friday to correct any suspicions that he had anything to do with the Smith boys' deaths.

The statement says that while he ended his relationship with Smith on October 18, a week before the boys' deaths, Findlay gave Smith a number of reasons for the breakup, including not being ready to be a father.

"However, that was far from the only reason for terminating the relationship and certainly was not the most important," the statement said. "At no time did I suggest to Ms. Smith that her children were the only obstacle in any potential relationship with her."

"Mr. Findlay has dated several people in the community," said spokeswoman Sharon O'Dell. "It was not a secret to people in the community that he was not ready to settle down into any serious relationship."

Thursday afternoon, Smith was arrested and charged with two counts of murder, after confessing to Union County Sheriff Howard Wells and SLED Chief Robert Stewart that she had killed her children. A coroner's report said they died from drowning.

Sources involved in the investigation said Friday there was no single event that broke open the investigation.

"I think inconsistencies in the things she said were what turned Smith into a key suspect," said SLED spokesman Hugh Munn. "They just kept confronting her."

One source said it was little things in Smith's stories that kept changing, like what happened at specific times.

In addition, a number of sources said Smith failed two lie detector tests – one given by the FBI and later one administered by SLED. The sources said on both occasions she failed when asked if she knew what had happened to her children.

On Friday morning, Smith buried her face into a coat, as police brought her to the Union County Courthouse to be arraigned for the murders of her children.

"Murderer, murderer murderer," chanted the crowd.

It was a scene far different from when she and her 24-year-old estranged husband, David, appealed to the nation for the safe return of their children, just a few days earlier.

"I'd hide my face, too," screamed Emily Griffith, a 43-year-old woman from Buffalo. "I didn't believe her from the start."

Edna Meadow, a 43-year-old black grandmother from Union, watched the throng of people gathered at the courthouse.

"It's not a race thing here," she said, referring to Smith's description of the man she said abducted her children. "It's about how those pitiful babies left this world."

Mrs. Meadow, a mother of six children, held her 3-year-old granddaughter, Whitney, while she spoke.

"My heart goes out to them babies," Mrs. Meadow said, as tears filled her eyes. "When you kill a child, you kill one of God's little angels."

Inside the courthouse Friday, Susan Smith chose to sit in jail rather than face the public in open court.

Smith remained behind closed doors while her newly retained attorney, David Bruck, appeared on her behalf.

Bruck, a well known death-penalty foe from Columbia, told Circuit Judge Larry R. Patterson of Greenville that he needed time to talk with Smith before requesting bond. The hearing lasted less than 10 minutes as about 150 reporters and on-lookers watched in the crowded courtroom.

Everyone going into the courtroom passed through a metal detector. Inside, SLED agents and Union County deputies lined the walls of the room.

Because of the public interest and difficulty in securing the courthouse, 16th Circuit Solicitor Thomas E. Pope, of Rock Hill, asked that the solicitor's office be given four days written notice before another hearing is called.

Bruck had little to say to the media after court but said his presence does not mean his client is involved in a capital case.

When asked about Smith's demeanor, however, Bruck stopped, paused and said, "Heartbroken."

Union county Sheriff Howard Wells said on a national television program Friday that Smith told him several times that she was very sorry and that she still loved her family and hoped they still loved her.

After court, Pope told the media that he will talk with the family and with community members before deciding whether to seek the death penalty.

In South Carolina, a death sentence can be ordered if a person is convicted of murdering more than one person or if the person murdered is younger that 12.

A grand jury is scheduled to meet Dec. 12 to consider an indictment against Smith, the next step in the legal process.

"I walked along Highway 49 for two days looking for something that would help the police find those little boys," said 45-year-old Mike Parks, who was outside the courthouse during Smith's hearing.

"I believed her right up to the end, but now, I feel betrayed."

About noon Friday, Gov. Carroll Campbell, acting on a request from Wells and Pope, ordered Smith to be taken from the York County Jail, where she was held Thursday night, to the Women's Correctional Facility in Columbia.

Smith will remain on a suicide watch through the weekend, a spokeswoman for the Corrections Department. She will not attend her children's funeral on Sunday.

"We are concerned about her safety," said spokeswoman Robyn Zimmerman. "We also don't let inmates go to victims' funerals."

Smith will be allowed to keep only her eye glasses, a Bible and a security blanket in her cell, which is 6 feet wide and 14 feet long.

Smith is under a suicide watch, Zimmerman said. In another safety measure, prison administrators will try to keep Smith in a cell isolated from other inmates. On Friday, there were 30 convicts in the prison's 48-cell solitary confinement unit, Zimmerman said.

"Inmates throughout our prison system are very angry, just as the general public is," she said.

Late Friday afternoon Margaret Gregory, a spokeswoman for the Smith family joined members of the Smith family in thanking people for the support they have received during the events that have forever changed their lives this week.

"An unimaginable event has ripped our lives apart, but we do stand here together as a family," said Gregory, speaking outside the courthouse, where angry on-lookers had gathered earlier in the day.

The scene on the other end of Main Street was more tranquil and sadder. Merchants took down a sea of yellow ribbons and replaced them with flowing ribbons of blue and white.

"The blue is for the little boys, and the white is for their innocence," said 21-year-old Carla Williams at The Pipe Rack, a Main Street clothing store. "Their mother made a fool out of everybody."

An evening prayer vigil at City Hall drew about 75 people.

It was Union's first day of healing.

Staff writer Molly McDonough and The (Columbia) State newspaper contributed to this report.

Herald-Journal, Spartanburg, South Carolina
Monday, November 7, 1994

'The boys are home'
Union says goodbye to Alex, Michael

By Gary Henderson
Staff Writer

BUFFALO - David Smith knelt to kiss his sons' snow-white casket just before it was lowered into the grave at Bogansville United Methodist Church cemetery Sunday afternoon.

"I don't want to leave; I don't want to leave," the 24-year-old father moaned as two family members helped him walk back to a waiting funeral service family car.

In the car, Smith clutched a photograph of 3-year-old Michael and 14-month-old Alex tightly to his chest, then fell forward in uncontrollable grief.

The scene was the end of a long day of mourning for the people of Union County, the state, and the nation.

In a county of 33,000 residents, police estimate 5,000 to 6,000 people participated in the services for the two children, who were found dead in their mother's submerged car at John D. Long Lake Thursday night.

"We were hoping it would not end this way," said Lt. Jeff Lawson of the Union County Sheriff's Office. Tears streamed down Lawson's face as he stood near the little boys' grave. "It was a long search."

The boys' bodies were found nine days after their mother, Susan V. Smith, falsely reported that she had been carjacked and that her sons had been abducted. After days of national media attention and several tearful appeals for the boys' return, Mrs. Smith confessed to authorities that she had killed her children.

The announcement caused a worldwide outpouring of grief. Gov. Carroll Campbell declared Sunday an official day of mourning in South Carolina, and well-wishers from as far away as New Zealand and Puerto Rico sent greetings to the bereaved family and the town of Union. Nearly 700 flower arrangements were sent to the services, including one from President Clinton.

At Buffalo United Methodist Church, site of the 2 p.m. funeral, mourners began arriving as early as 6 a.m.

By 11:30 Sunday morning, a long line had already formed outside. Speakers were placed outdoors and in the church dining room so the overflow crowd could hear the service, though the ministers' voices often were obscured by a whirring news helicopter and the hum of TV crews' diesel generators.

About 70 miles away, the boys' mother spent the day alone in her cell at the Women's Correctional Facility in Columbia. Prison officials said Mrs. Smith did not ask for a television set to watch the reports of her sons' funeral, nor did she attend worship services or speak with a pastor.

South Carolina Department of Corrections spokeswoman Robyn Zimmerman said Mrs. Smith, who has been charged with two counts of murder, remained under a suicide watch in solitary confinement.

Just before 1 p.m., the casket containing both boys' bodies was rolled to the front of the Buffalo church. Ushers allowed people who were not able to get a seat to come inside the church for a last visit with the children.

For more than an hour, a steady stream of people walked to the front of the church. Some of them touched the casket. All of them wept.

One elderly woman drove all night from northern Virginia to attend Sunday's services.

"I lost twins when they were 16-years-old," said Ferroll Craig of Newport News, Va. "It hurts so much to see these young lives snuffed out so needlessly. I was compelled to be here. God wants me here."

Robert Brand and his family from Stone Mountain, Ga., also were drawn to Union County.

"We really couldn't believe this could happen to those two little boys. For us, this makes it real," Brand said as he stood in the churchyard during the funeral. "We just had to come and say good-bye to those two little boys."

Brand, his wife Ayesha, and two sons, Omar, 4, and Zarief, 5, made the four-hour journey on the spur of the moment.

"We were on our way to church this morning when we just decided we had to be here," Brand said. "It was worth the trip."

A Charlotte woman with her own 14-month-old baby in her arms stood alone on the grass near the church and cried. "It still hurts," said Christine Alexander. "I know we're supposed to forgive (Mrs. Smith), but I can't."

Keith and Carmine Segars of Greenville, prayed with their two children, Jonathan, 4, and Tiffany, 6. Attending the service, they said, was a way of showing support for the family the boys left behind.

The couple said their children understand the basics of what happened, but have questions that no one can answer.

"They're asking for answers, and I have no answers to give," Mrs. Segars said. "How do you explain this?"

Inside the church, many mourners communicated with a look or a touch instead of words.

Just before the funeral began, two little boys walked to the front of the church and stared briefly at the photograph of Michael and Alex Smith that rested on the white casket. Then the older boy reached down and took his companion's hand as the two of them left the church in silence.

While every moment of the funeral was filled with expressions of grief and sorrow, there were two times when the emotions were overwhelming.

When the music-box sounds of "Jesus Loves Me" and "Away In A Manger" were played, few people were able to hold back the tears.

"The boys won't be here for Christmas," a woman said softly at the rear of the sanctuary.

The Rev. Bob Cato of Union struggled with words as he spoke at the service.

"Last Tuesday night, I met with David and his family," Cato said "They said, 'We want our boys home.' "

Cato paused.

"The boys are home."

David Smith walked behind his sons' casket as it was rolled from the church and loaded into a steel-gray hearse for the 7-mile ride to Bogansville United Methodist Church Cemetery in West Springs. Before he got into the car, the distraught man turned for a final look at his sons' rose-draped casket.

The trip west along Highway 215 was like a final salute to Michael and Alex.

Almost every mailbox was draped in blue ribbons. People stood in the yards or sat on porches to watch as Michael and Alex passed. Some held signs that said, "We love you and will never forget you, Alex and Michael."

Just outside the farm village of Putnam, where David and Susan lived when they were first married, a man and a boy stood silently by the road. The little boy held a large bouquet of helium-filled blue and white balloons.

"Alex and Michael died on my birthday," said Carrie Waite, a 35-year-old woman from Chattanooga, Tenn. "I don't know why, but I had to come here. I'll always have a reminder of them every year."

As the final prayer at the graveside services ended, two soft-blue balloons drifted toward the heavens.

While the crowd of nearly 2,000 dispersed from the cemetery, Dr. Mark Long, pastor of Buffalo United Methodist Church, tried to put the day's events into perspective.

"My message to David and the world is one of hope," Long said. "Through God, we are able to overcome this. David Smith will need your prayers. A big chunk of his life has been buried here today."

David Smith's friends and neighbors said they, too, will take time to heal.

"All these people that came here, they'll go away. But for we that live here, this is hard." said Elizabeth Kingsmore, 80, of Buffalo. "It's going to stay with us. We'll try to forget, but it will be hard."

Her grandson, David, agreed. "This is the worst thing that's happened to this town since the Civil War," he said. "This leaves a lot of hurt."

Staff writer Chase Squires contributed to this report.

MORE GOOD BOOKS FROM HONORIBUS PRESS

THIS IS YOUR ORDER FORM
JUST CLIP and MAIL

_____ **VALLEY OF THE SHADOW** $4.95
Ed. Y. Hall.
The Vietnam War. A young army officer's combat tour as an
Advisor with the South Vietnamese Army. Introduction
by Gen. William C. Westmoreland. 1966-67.
ISBN 0-9622166-0-7

_____ **FLYING WITH THE HELL'S ANGELS** $5.95
Samuel P. Fleming as told to Ed. Y. Hall.
Memoirs of an Eighth Air Force Navigator's 30 missions over
Fortress Europe with the 303rd Bombardment Group. 1943-1944.
ISBN 0-9622166-1-5

_____ **UNPUBLISHED ACTIVITIES OF WORLD WAR II** $16.95
Earl J. Roberts.
Frontline duty with the infantry in Europe during
World War II with the 187th Infantry Regiment. 1944-1945.
Hard Cover. ISBN 940553-00-7

_____ **FATED TO SURVIVE** $7.50
William P. Maher, Edited by Ed. Y. Hall.
Memoirs of an Eighth Air Force B-17 Pilot / POW.
401st Bomb Group. 1943-1945. ISBN 0-9622166-2-3

_____ **THE SEARCH FOR MIAs** $12.95
Garry L. Smith, Edited by Ed. Y. Hall.
Answers to the question of "What happened to our Vietnam War
unaccounted for POWs and MIAs?"
Soft Cover. ISBN 0-9622166-3-1

_____ **HARRIET QUIMBY –** $12.95
AMERICA'S FIRST LADY OF THE AIR
Ed. Y. Hall.
The tragic life of America's first licensed woman pilot, and the
first woman to pilot an aircraft across the English Channel
1875-1912. Soft Cover. ISBN 0-9622166-4-X

_____ **HARRIET QUIMBY –** $4.95
AN ACTIVITY BOOK FOR CHILDREN
Anita P. Davis / Ed. Y. Hall.
A companion activity work book for children (ages 10-14)
to the book *Harriet Quimby – America's First Lady of the Air.*
Soft Cover. ISBN 0-9622166-3-8

(TURN PAGE FOR MORE GOOD BOOKS)

_____	COMBAT SURGEON	$12.95

      Dr. William C. Herbert, Jr. M.D.
      Memoirs of a U.S. Army Medical Corps Officer
      in Europe during World War II. Soft Cover.
      ISBN 0-9622166-6-6

_____	DIVISION COMMANDER – A BIOGRAPHY	$18.95

      OF MAJOR GENERAL NORMAN D. COTA
      Robert A. Miller.
      An exciting biography of a true hero of World War II.
      A "fighting general" whose wartime record reads like a
      resume of the Mediterranean and European campaigns.
      Hard Cover. ISBN 0-87152-438-4

_____	NINE DAYS IN UNION –	$12.95

      THE SEARCH FOR ALEX AND MICHAEL SMITH
      Gary Henderson.
      Behind the scenes, award winning story with Henderson and
      Herald-Journal photographer Mike Bonner during the nine day
      national search for the missing Smith boys.
      Soft Cover. ISBN 1-883534-00-2

TO ORDER

Please check the space next to the book(s) you want, send this order form together with your check or money order, include the price of the book(s) and add $2.00 for the first book and $1.00 for each additional book for handling and mailing to:

HONORIBUS PRESS
P.O. BOX 4872
SPARTANBURG, SC 29305

I have enclosed $ _____ Check _____ or money order as payment in full. Please no COD's.

Name _____

Address_____

City _____

State _____ Zip _____

Please allow 2-3 weeks for delivery.